BEING TRUE
TO
YOURSELF

A Multidimensional Approach
for Seasoned Travelers on the Spiritual Path

BEING TRUE
TO
YOURSELF

A Multidimensional Approach
for Seasoned Travelers on the Spiritual Path

LINDA MARY ROBINSON

Personal Pathways of Light
Hampton, VA

Being True to Yourself
A Multidimensional Approach for Seasoned Travelers on the Spiritual Path

Published by:
Personal Pathways of Light
26 Towne Centre Way, #184
Hampton, VA 23666 USA
www.PersonalPathwaysOfLight.com

ISBN: 978-0-9915497-2-6

Library of Congress Control Number: 2019907796

Editor: Cheryl Cease Williams

Printed in the United States of America

This book is dedicated to the Beings of Light in the Higher Realms, who are always there for us when we call on them.

I would like to thank all of my Soul Family for your support, encouragement, assistance, and insights throughout my spiritual journey, and especially during the writing of this book. I treasure the times we have shared together and look forward to many more with you. You are precious Lights on my path.

Contents

Preface

———✂——

The Beings of Light bring us much wisdom from the Higher Realms. Their teachings cover a wide range of subjects to invite us on the Earth Plane to view things from a different and, often, higher perspective.

As a seasoned traveler on the spiritual path, you are likely to be well-acquainted with receiving your own guidance from the Higher Realms, whether it comes in the form of a passing thought or a more direct prompting or channeling. This is a natural occurrence for those who are in close communication with the Beings of Light across the veil.

This book includes wisdom teachings I have received from the Higher Realms, with a focus on the messages from Archangel Zadkiel and Lady Amethyst and others in the Angelic Realm of Light. The Ascended Masters, the Divine Feminine, the Hathors, the Star Beings, and my Higher Self also gave inspiration for the topics of discussion. Many of the chapters include a message from the Angelic Realm. I am very grateful to the Beings of Light who have brought me these wisdom teachings and who continue to work with me.

As an added emphasis, Zadkiel and Lady Amethyst are the Archangels on the Seventh Ray of Light, which is also the home of Ascended Masters Saint Germain and Lady Portia, and the Violet Flame. This Ray is particularly important at this time because it focuses on transmutation, transformation, and manifestation. It is of special significance as many of us are transforming our spiritual paths to be true to ourselves as we move higher on the spiral of ascension.

Some of the concepts in this book may be discussed more than once. This is not an oversight, but it is rather to emphasize the importance of that information. When this occurs, I have been prompted by the Higher Beings to include these concepts in this way.

I have also included my personal experiences and how I have applied the teachings I received. The beauty of the wisdom teachings is that you can individualize them to your own circumstances and where you are on your path.

Each chapter will include a concept for consideration, and it will be like a strand of Light going from the basic level to the multidimensional and beyond.

My use of the term multidimensional denotes that the Universe is composed of many levels. Each one flows into the next. You may view this as an upward movement or as the dimensions interpenetrating or superimposed on each other. Your own perception will guide you on the interpretation that is right for you.

We on the Earth Plane have been living in the third dimension for many years. However, as seasoned travelers on the spiritual path, we have experienced many dimensions beyond this. We are capable of understanding and functioning on more than one level at a time. When we open ourselves to this understanding and expression, we move higher on our ascension path. Let your imagination and guidance allow you to flow to your next level of growth.

My personal belief is that we all originated from the Great Creator or Source. In this book, I will interchangeably use a variety of terms for this Point of Creation, including God, Source, Creator, Universe, All That Is, etc. Whenever you read the term that I have used, please substitute your own term that resonates with you and your path.

I will share a variety of ideas in this book. I am writing it for you and where you are on your path and to inspire you to be true to yourself. If you find that some of the ideas resonate with you, then you can choose them for further consideration. If you find others that don't resonate with you or your belief system, simply leave them alone and instead focus on those things that do resonate with you. Above all, be true to yourself!

Introduction

Being on a spiritual path is very exciting and fulfilling. As a seasoned traveler on the path, you have made great strides in your ascension process. You have developed a great understanding of the process needed for spiritual enlightenment, and you have shared this with others on their journey of awakening, whether you are a healer, teacher, author, or fellow Lightworker.

You have taken a bold step to walk your own path in a world that wants many of us to conform.

Now it is your time to refocus on yourself to see if you want to make any adjustments on a personal or professional level.

You may have experienced a realization, as I did, that certain parts of your path no longer bring you the joy they once did, or you may have hit rough patches along the way. This may have happened all at once, or it may have developed as a growing awareness that something needed to be changed or adjusted. This is a sign that you have progressed to another spiritual level. When this occurs, taking a fresh look at your spiritual practices and work can help you pinpoint if there are any changes you want to make.

In this book, I will share with you what I learned as I experienced the inner prompt to look more deeply at my path and to make adjustments along the way. In this process, I learned that I am continually changing and evolving. What was true for me yesterday may be different today.

I will interweave the wisdom teachings I have received from the Angelic Realm along with my own personal experiences as I took each step to remain true to myself on my path.

It is an honor, a privilege, and a great joy to inspire you and share these wisdom teachings and my journey with you as you are being true to yourself on your path.

Back at Square One ... At a Higher Level

I was back at square one. I thought I had made so much progress in knowing what was right for me and being true to myself.

Early in my spiritual journey, I was like a child in a candy store. There were so many things to do, books to read, and classes to take. I explored everything I could fit into my schedule. I was still working in my previous career as an educator teaching life skills to adults and youth, so I participated in spiritual activities any time I wasn't working.

After I retired from that career, I began to take even more classes. There didn't seem to be enough hours in the day for what I wanted to do. As I described in my first book, *Reflections on the Path: The Awakening*, my guides and teachers gave me many lessons on choosing wisely and being true to myself.

At that time, I heeded their advice. I pruned away many activities that I had enjoyed but weren't truly at the core of my desire to inspire others on their spiritual path.

I thought I had mastered that lesson.

But how wrong I was!

For several years I had kept my focus on teaching and speaking on wisdom teachings from the Angelic Realm and channeling monthly messages from Archangel Zadkiel and Lady Amethyst for my website. I also participated in spiritual pilgrimages to many countries and sacred sites that enhanced my understanding of my path.

And I continued to take classes. Each time I heard about another class, I signed up and participated. Even if I didn't feel particularly called to the specific topic of the class, I took it anyway, especially if those I considered to be spiritually advanced were taking it. I thought maybe that particular class would provide the answer I was looking for. Maybe it would be the thing that propelled me to the next level.

With the advent of online classes, I felt myself being pulled to try to take as many classes as I could. After all, I could do that from the comfort of my home! It was simply not enough for me only to attend classes in person.

Social media added to the feeling of being pulled in too many directions. As I read about what classes others were taking, especially those persons who were on an advanced spiritual path, I wondered whether I, too, needed to take those classes. Maybe that would make me more spiritual, or maybe I couldn't be as spiritual as I wanted to be if I didn't take those classes or pursue that type of path. I felt that I "should" be taking these classes because, after all, wasn't that what a spiritual person "should" do?

At times, I felt as if I might be losing my way or my direction on my spiritual path. I even questioned who I was, what I really wanted, and what I was supposed to be doing.

One day after I returned from taking a class, I realized that, once again, I had let myself stray from my focus and purpose.

Suddenly, I realized I was overloaded. I felt overwhelmed.

Exhausted from it all, I sat down in my favorite meditation spot and began to reflect. How had this happened? Didn't I learn my lesson years earlier? How had I allowed myself to get into this situation again?

As I settled into my quiet spot, I heard the voice of one of my earliest teachers saying, "Remember, you can't do it all."

Then I recalled the lessons from my guides encouraging me to choose wisely and select those things that were most important to me and, above all, to be true to myself.

How could I have forgotten those lessons? Why did I not continue to apply them to my own path?

Then my guides came in and said, "When you

move to another level of mastery, the same lessons may appear again to see if you have truly mastered them or if there is still work to do."

Clearly, I still had work to do on the lesson of being true to myself on my path.

I took a deep sigh of relief as I realized I didn't have to do it all. The Higher Realms weren't expecting me or anyone else to do it all. They wanted me to be true to myself and to do what made my heart sing.

I was beginning that lesson again at a higher dimension of understanding.

A Lesson in Being True to Myself

Where could I start on this new phase of understanding? What did it mean to me to be true to myself on my path?

My mind drifted back to the messages I had received from Archangel Zadkiel and Lady Amethyst and had posted on my website, www.PersonalPathwaysOfLight.com. As I began to look at them, I got excited as I realized that I had been given teachings on this subject for the last several years.

As I looked back at the messages and reflected on my path during that time, I could see how the messages and my path were a story that intertwined the teachings with my experiences. They would be a perfect blend for my book.

I started off with high expectations of completing this book quickly. After all, I already had the channeled messages/teachings, so I felt that this would be easy to complete.

When I began writing the book, I followed a format that many others had used successfully. But it didn't feel right for me for this book. Something was missing, so I set the project aside and wondered whether I was really supposed to write this book.

Then, one day the answer came through like a thunderbolt. Once again, I was trying to follow someone else's path. I wasn't excited, and I felt a sense of dread whenever I sat down to work on it. I later discovered that feeling a sense of dread was one of my signals that I wasn't being true to myself. The cookie-cutter approach didn't make my heart sing.

As I continued to work through this process, I decided to take excerpts from selected messages and interweave them as appropriate with my experiences and some of my other writings that my guides were prompting me to include. I needed to put my heart and soul into my writing. I needed to make the book mine.

As I began selecting messages to include, I realized that some of them were being updated by a composite group of the Higher Beings of Light. The updating of the messages reflected the constantly changing, higher vibrational energy. The messages even began to shift from a third-dimensional linear perspective to one of a multidimensional approach. The Beings of Light told me that with this incoming higher vibrational energy, we are constantly being given the opportunity to change along with it and that it is important to remain in the flow.

I felt a freshness and aliveness when this occurred. I was being true to the most current version of myself.

Join Me as We Explore!

In this book, *Being True to Yourself: A Multidimensional Approach for Seasoned Travelers on the Spiritual Path*, I will be discussing ideas for consideration and interweaving my experiences along with excerpts from some of the channeled messages and wisdom teachings I have received that illustrate the lessons I needed at each point to help me remain true to myself.

As you read these messages and experiences, I invite you to reflect on your own journey and join me as we explore being true to yourself on your path!

PART 1

REALIZING YOUR PATH
IS NO LONGER YOU

How Did I Get Here?

—∽⟨⟩∾—

At this point, you may be questioning whether you are being true to yourself on your spiritual path. You have made much progress and accomplished a great deal. But still you may be wondering whether there is something more you would like to do or be. You may even be asking yourself if this is all there is.

Although your current path has previously brought you joy and fulfillment, it may now feel stale. You want something different.

If your current path has consumed all of your time, you may even be feeling resentful that you have no free and unstructured time for yourself. You want to get off the whirling circle that now feels more confining rather than fulfilling.

You may want to explore new interests, or you may just want to be.

Having time just to be rather than always doing

something, or thinking that you need to be doing something, is a feeling that many seasoned travelers on the spiritual path are experiencing. You may be feeling that you have given of yourself for so long, and you are asking yourself, "When will it be my time for me?"

These are all signs that you have progressed to a new and higher level.

You want to make a change, but how do you do it?

You may have clients or friends who are urging you to continue your current path and activities. You don't want to disappoint them, but still it is harder and harder for you to put on a happy face each day and have genuine excitement about what you are doing.

Even more concerning, how do you change and not risk a loss of clients or friends and a potential impact on your income or social life?

Would you make a change if money or friendship were of no concern?

Will your change make a difference in how others view you? Will this matter to you?

Do you feel that you need permission to change?

Where do you start in the process of discovering

who you are at this point on your journey?

How do you get to the next step and level on your path and remain true to yourself?

You Are Special

The questions about how you got to your current stage can be perplexing.

Before you dive in to get these answers for yourself, it may be helpful for you to reflect on just how special you are.

You are a shining thread in the beautiful tapestry of the cosmos. You have a special mission and role for your own ascension and for the greater good of all of humanity.

Before you came into this incarnation, you made a contract with your guides about what you wanted to accomplish in this lifetime. It may have been something large such as being a great leader, or it may have been something on a more local level where you were an inspiration to others through the way you conducted yourself in daily life. No matter what you agreed to, it was done for your highest good and the greatest good of all.

In order to accomplish your mission, you were given exactly what you would need for this great adventure. You have unique talents and abilities that are tailored for your special mission. No one else has the exact same set of abilities that you have.

You may already know what your special gifts and talents are, or you may find yourself asking what they are.

If you are unsure what they are, dig deep into your inner being, and your heart will reveal them to you. This may come in the form of a yearning for that something greater, a vision of what you see yourself doing in your wildest dreams, or a prompt from what someone says. You may see someone else doing something and say to yourself, "I would love to do that!"

You may even decide to ask yourself a series of questions to help you focus on your special gifts.

For example, do you take charge when you are involved in a group project? If so, you may be a natural leader.

Are you the one who everyone wants to confide in? If so, you may be a caring, compassionate listener.

Do you enjoy showing others how to do things? If so, you may be a teacher on many levels, not just in a classroom setting.

What are you happiest doing?

As I thought about my gifts and talents, I realized that I enjoy sharing with others what I have learned. This comes in the form of teaching classes, speaking, and writing. I also love listening to others. I am happiest when I am sharing with others and listening to their insights.

As you ponder your responses to the questions you have asked yourself, your natural talents and abilities will be revealed to you.

Your life experiences, special talents, and the skills and abilities you have developed all contribute to the unique person you are.

As you honor and appreciate your own gifts and talents, they will continue to grow and radiate forth as a beacon to others.

Just as threads of many colors form a beautiful tapestry, so do the pathways and missions of individuals form a supportive network of growth and ascension for humanity. When you are true to yourself, you are able to carry out your mission for the greatest good of all.

Love and appreciate your own gifts and talents, for you have a unique path and role to play in the cosmos. Love yourself, honor yourself, and be true to yourself, for you are truly special!

◆ ◆ ◆

Your Unique Mission

~ Inspiration from The Angelic Realm ~

Beloved Ones,

Indeed, this is a most auspicious time for you in your personal journey as well as for your beloved planet and Universe.

This is a time where you are needed in your fullest capacity. You brought forth with you in this lifetime the potential to manifest great gifts that would benefit not only yourself but all of mankind. The planet and mankind are reaching a point where critical mass is needed to affect the great shift that has long been predicted.

Your particular talents and blend of abilities are unique to you. Others may have similar ones, but they are not in the same proportion or in the same array. You agreed to come forth with your special gifts and to be in your particular location in order to play a very important role in the ascension of humanity and the planet. Everything is on schedule for the ascension, and this is the time for you to manifest your gifts for your greatest good and the highest good of all. Indeed, you are a shining jewel in the grand plan for humanity.

In order for you to bring forth your talents and abilities in the greatest measure, we would ask you to focus on what your gifts and abilities are. They may be that you are a caring person who is good at working with others. You may be one who has a special talent for working with plants or animals or the mineral kingdom. Whatever your special area is, it is one that was designed for you and which you agreed to carry out.

Many circumstances occur in your life that are part of the grander scheme for humanity and the planet. When certain things occur, you may wonder why you were in that particular place at that particular time. Beloveds, it is because you have agreed to this, and you paid attention to the nudges of your Soul to be at a certain place or to talk to a particular person at that time.

When you view events from a higher perspective, you can see how all of the interactions and events form a beautiful tapestry and picture. If you think of the bigger picture as a beautiful tapestry, you can see how your particular thread contributes to the bigger picture and the beauty of the whole. If you were to remove your particular thread from the tapestry, the quality of the entire piece would be changed. Something would be missing.

It is the same with your unique talents and abilities. If you were to remove your particular blend of gifts from humanity, there would be a noticeable hole or bare spot left where your gifts had been. This is why it is especially important in these times that each person step forward with their own unique gifts to contribute to the greater good of all.

As you use your gifts and talents for your greatest good and the highest good of all, you can feel your vibration begin to resonate in harmony because you are performing your unique contribution. It is those things that make your heart sing. It is not about trying to copy what someone else is doing. It is about doing those things that you really enjoy, those things in which you know you excel, and those things that make life better for everyone.

When you perfect your own skills and abilities and use them in this way, your vibration increases, and you begin to rise higher on your ascension path. You begin to appreciate your own gifts and to recognize the gifts that others are contributing. You begin to see that each person is unique and has a contribution to make. Whatever your station is in life, you are unique and contribute to the betterment of all.

The important part for you to remember is to appreciate yourself and your own gifts first. Focus on what you do that makes the world a better place for all of humanity. Look deeper within yourself and see your own Divine Spark that connects you to Source. Realize that your gifts and abilities are a reflection of your Divine Spark. Give thanks and appreciation for having been given these gifts and for the opportunity to use them for the betterment of all.

As you look deeper within, you will feel your Divine connection. A feeling of Love and gratitude will begin to wash over you as you realize the grand scheme of everyone playing their part for the greater good of all. You will realize that each person is contributing to the betterment of humanity, and you will have a greater appreciation for your own role and your own gifts and abilities.

Focusing on these feelings will allow you to form an even deeper connection with All That Is. You will realize that each person is part of the greater Whole. As you go throughout your daily life, you will see how each person makes your own life better because of their unique contributions. When you express appreciation to them for what they do, it not only raises their vibration, it also raises your own, for you understand that each person plays a role in helping humanity to ascend.

Before you go to sleep each night, think of the ways that you have helped others that day and of the ways that others have helped you. Think about how you and each of the others have played a unique part in making the world a better place for everyone.

When you arise in the morning, take a moment to focus on your unique talents and abilities and ask that you use them throughout the day for the betterment of humanity and the planet. Ask that you look for the good in others and express appreciation for what they do.

As you think about the appreciation you have for others, remember to ask for the highest and best for all concerned.

Call on us, and we are with you.

Know that you are greatly loved.

~ The Angelic Realm

To Thine Own Self Be True

—⟨∞⟩—

You have focused on your special qualities and your mission.

At this point you may be thinking, "This all sounds good, but what exactly does that have to do with being true to myself, especially since I am a seasoned traveler on the spiritual path?" Do you say, "I 'should' already have this," and then beat up on yourself? Often, we do this very thing to ourselves.

"To Thine Own Self Be True." These words by William Shakespeare are just as true today as they were when Shakespeare first wrote them.

Remaining true to yourself is very important when you walk your path. You want to be certain that the path you are walking is your own at your current point of ascension. You do not want to walk someone else's path or yield to their desire for what they want you to do, unless it is yours also.

Determining who you are and what you want at every step of the way is a prerequisite for getting the most from your path.

It is not a one-time occurrence but rather an ongoing process in which you listen to your inner guidance and feelings all along the way.

There are many ways for your inner guidance to appear. You may have a knowing in your mind. You may have a feeling in your heart. You may see a book, a billboard, a television show, or a meaningful sequence of numbers such as 111 or 444 that prompts you. At this point on your path, you probably have your own favorites or "go-to" techniques.

For me, a knowing forms in my mind. This is followed by a validation at my heart level that brings a feeling of peace.

Sometimes, I receive an additional validation.

On one occasion, this occurred when I was writing. I was describing a particular concept, and one of my guides who is an Ascended Master appeared in my mind's eye and gave me a suggestion about what to add and how to phrase it. Because he had worked with me previously on my writing, I paused to reflect on his suggestion. It felt right, and I continued to move forward. That night, as I was preparing for sleep, I decided to pull a card from one of my favorite spiritual card decks. I asked a question that always yields good advice for me ... "Tell me what I need to know." Amazingly, I drew the card of the Ascended Master who had worked with me earlier. I was elated! I had received an additional validation.

There are many methods for receiving and verifying your inner prompts. The one you select is valid for you. Your method doesn't have to be the same as someone else's. The important thing is to be aware of how you receive your inner prompts and to pay attention when they appear.

It is your decision as to what your next step will be. If you find that you have taken a step that doesn't resonate with you, then you can make a correction or adjustment in your path so that it does feel like you.

Sometimes you may say, "I don't know what I want." This is a common occurrence if you have often listened to what others want and have allowed their wishes to supersede your own. Many times you may have found it easier to go along with the crowd than to step out on your own.

If that is the case, don't beat yourself up. This is a

time where we need to be very gentle with ourselves and realize that we have been doing our best all along the journey. Everything is a learning experience. There is still an opportunity for you to be true to yourself on your path.

Each moment is a new beginning.

◆ ◆ ◆

Your Special Path

~ Inspiration from The Angelic Realm ~

Beloved Ones,

You are a unique Being of Light. You burst forth from the Creator with Love and Light. You contained all of the universal aspects and attributes needed to help you carry out your special mission. Throughout your many incarnations, you have continued to develop special qualities, and you have used them for the greatest good of all.

Each individual has a unique mission and path. In each incarnation you have carried out your special mission. This has led you to develop many additional qualities and attributes that are contributing to your mission and to the greatest

34

good throughout the multidimensions.

You have used these qualities in each lifetime as you have moved along your path. You are playing your special part in the great tapestry of life and universal creation.

Each lifetime can be considered to be a series of stepping stones. Each step leads to the next. When you focus on each step as it occurs, you are able to gain the experience and receive the signals that will lead you to the next one. Each step is part of your unique path and your contribution to the greater good.

Therefore, it is important for you to remain true to your special path.

You are presented with many possibilities as you go along your path. These may appear as a fork in the road where choices can be made. They may also appear as many opportunities being presented at one time. Each option represents a direction on your path. These are not to be viewed as good or bad, but rather as a selection of which choice is the right fit for you at that time. The choice you make will help determine the next step on your path and can also influence future directions.

Therefore, it is helpful to be in tune with who you are and what you feel you would like your contribution to the greater good to be. Because each person is different, this is a very individual decision.

This can be exciting for you because it allows you to tap into your potential and do what your heart desires.

You may have known from an early age what your heart desired, or you may have had several options that called to you. Whatever the case, it is sometimes helpful to pause and reflect on where you are on your path.

One of the first assessments is to determine whether your direction makes your heart sing. You may wish to set aside some quiet time and think about your path and next step. Tune in to your heart and see how you feel when you think about or picture your next step. Do you feel happy and joyous? If so, this may be an indication that this is a fit for your special path. If you do not feel joyous, you can focus on each part of the next step to try to isolate which part does not make you feel happy and whether you may want to modify it.

By doing this regularly, you are more likely to stay true to your special path.

Another aspect to review is to determine whether the next step on your path is for highest good. You are now living in an era where you recognize that everyone and everything are connected. Your path is part of the greater tapestry of creation, and everything affects everything else. When your next step is in alignment with greatest good, everyone benefits, and you move forward in a flowing manner.

Remaining in the present moment can also help you in taking your next step. You recognize changes in circumstances that will help you know whether you wish to make an adjustment, or you may see signs that affirm that your next step is where you wish to be.

These signs may include a book you read, something you see on television, or a conversation with someone. You may see a feather or other object in nature or an animal that is special to you. When you remain in the present moment, you are able to recognize the signals as they occur.

Honoring yourself by regularly taking this quiet

time to review your next step can help you do what makes your heart sing while being of service for greatest good.

Know that you are greatly loved.

~ The Angelic Realm

The Balancing Act of Being True to Yourself

Why is it so hard to be true to yourself in these times? We may feel like a square peg trying to fit into a round hole. Advertising tries to persuade us to be a certain way ... to wear certain clothes, to drive a particular car, and to eat specific foods. Social media highlights persons who are successful and advanced on their spiritual journey. Retreats and classes are being promoted. Well-meaning friends claim that they have found the path to enlightenment. We are constantly being bombarded with all sorts of possibilities, many of which conflict with each other and send mixed messages. It is not surprising that we wake up one day and wonder who we are, who our authentic self is, and what we truly want for our next step.

This is actually a hopeful sign because now you are ready to sort out what is right for you and what you want to discard. You are on a journey of continuing to discover your true self.

Claiming your authentic self can be daunting, especially if you are going against the accepted norms of your family, community, workplace, or other spiritual friends. You may feel alienated from those closest to you. It is a decision to be made with much care and weighing the pros and cons of the choice.

Are you more comfortable staying within the confines of accepted norms, or do you want to venture outside them? Only you can decide.

The flip side of the challenges in being true to yourself is that there are also many opportunities for self-exploration. In previous decades, the choices were more limited.

You may have been expected to follow a certain career, a family tradition, or a religious path. Each geographic location may have had certain norms that were hard to ignore.

Those choices served their purpose for the times in which they were created. However, as times changed, the need for a wider range of possibilities emerged.

For me, I stayed in the shadows for a long time.

I grew up in the 1950s and 1960s in a community where there were many expectations of what was "right" and "proper." Having the approval of the community and adhering to its norms were paramount in my small, rural, conservative, Southern upbringing in the United States.

I often felt like a square peg in a round hole. My heart yearned for adventure.

At that time options for women were limited. Careers were very traditional, and women were expected to acquiesce to the expectations of society. A career for a woman was often considered a sideline and took second place to the needs of others.

Religious paths were also very traditional. I had never been exposed to beliefs and philosophies outside mainstream religion until I moved to Virginia and became acquainted with metaphysical bookstores and organizations.

There I found expanded views of traditional religion and other philosophies that called to my heart. I felt that I had found my true home and calling to be of service to an expanded view of spirituality and consciousness.

For a long time, I kept my path of study close to

my own small group of like-minded friends.

I knew that I would face disapproval from many sources if I revealed my spiritual path of metaphysics, Oneness, and working with the Angelic Realm, the Ascended Masters, and other Higher Beings of Light.

When I wrote my first book, *Reflections on the Path: The Awakening*, in which I described my spiritual awakening and channeling work with the Higher Realms, I only told those who were supportive of my work. I wasn't ready to face disapproval from those whose approval I wanted. Those I told received it well, and I gained the courage to list it on my website, www.PersonalPathwaysOfLight.com, which I also had only revealed to like-minded people.

As I began writing this book, I realized that I was more comfortable describing my spiritual path than I had been previously. This has been part of my own spiritual growth of not being as concerned about the approval of others. Now when I talk about my path, I can be of greater service and more effectively provide inspiration as I describe how I arrived at my current point of understanding. I respect and honor that others may be on a different path. I only ask that they honor and respect the path I have chosen. When we honor and respect each other, we all grow exponentially.

We are now living in a time where there are many opportunities. Options on the spiritual path have expanded. If something doesn't resonate with us, there are other options available.

You continue to be a unique individual. You no longer have to fit into a mold that isn't you.

You can explore what makes your heart sing.

◆ ◆ ◆

Standing in Your Truth

~ Inspiration from The Angelic Realm ~

Beloved Ones,

You are making great strides in the new energy. You have experienced extraordinary leaps in consciousness, and your awareness has opened to new vistas. You have radiated your Light for all to see.

The new energy has presented many opportunities for you to examine all aspects of your Being and to release those aspects that are no longer part of your multidimensional Self. Now, you are poised to continue to open to even greater levels of awareness in this new energy.

Standing in your truth is an important part of the new energy. This is one of the many changes that have come with the new energy. You are being given the opportunity to examine yourself and your choices and to decide what your new ones will be. Being in the midst of shifting energy is much easier when you stand in your own truth.

The herd mentality of expecting everyone to follow the same path is fading. This is a time of individual growth and great enlightenment.

You are being given a great opportunity to decide what is really important to you. When you are clear about what this is, you can move forward with the assurance and confidence of being true to yourself at a core level.

This can bring a great peace to you because you are living from the core of your Being – from that central, inner part of yourself that is in harmony with All That Is. It is that part of you that is loving and caring and expresses those attributes first to yourself and then to others. When you stand in your truth, you treat yourself with the same consideration that you would give someone else. You treat yourself with respect. You honor yourself for the way in which you are moving forward. You

*become your best friend and supporter. You focus
on your positive attributes and build on them.*

*For example, you may be kind and compassionate.
As you are kind and compassionate with yourself,
you are able to extend these qualities to others. The
more you focus on these attributes, the stronger
they become. What you focus on expands. As you
strengthen your positive inner qualities, you
become stronger. Your inner core Being is self-
assured, and you know that you are making choices
that honor who you are.*

*As you move more fully into the new energy, you
may wish to reflect on what your core values are.
They are who you are and determine what decisions
you make and what actions flow from them.*

*Core values can be qualities such as honesty,
loyalty, respect, love, caring, and many others.
These are the things that are the core of your Being.
These are the things that sustain you when
conditions around you are changing. They allow
you to move forward and know that you are being
who you really are. They provide a source of
strength and steadiness. They provide an assurance
to you to maintain who you are even when you are
around others with different viewpoints. You*

become comfortable with others having different views, and you still remain centered because you have an inner assurance of who you are. You are standing in your truth.

When you relax into your truth, you can experience a peacefulness that comes from knowing that you are being your authentic self. You are walking your talk. This allows you to flow and be in the present moment. You gain new insights that often seem to be synchronistic. This can occur because you are on an energetic vibration that resonates with these insights. Because you are standing in your truth, you are open to receive. You are in a state of harmony with All That Is.

You are powerful when you stand in your truth. When you can do this and also allow others to stand in their truth, you are even more powerful. You are moving into a time where individuality combined with respect, honor, and compassion for others is increasingly important.

As you move forward on your path, standing in your truth, along with having respect and compassion for others, can assist you in carrying out your role in helping to lift the consciousness of humanity. You are serving as a Way-Shower and a

Light-Bearer through your daily actions.

You see the bigger picture and ask for highest good. This opens up avenues of higher consciousness, and you are able to be of even greater service.

Know that you are greatly loved.

~ The Angelic Realm

Listening to the Song of Your Heart

———✕❍✕———

What makes your heart sing?

You may have your favorite way to decide what you want. You may be one of those fortunate persons who can easily determine what is right for you. Or you may be someone who needs a little more time to discern what is right for you ... what is really you as opposed to what you think you are supposed to do or what others expect you to do. Or you may be one who has processed your path mentally without considering your feelings.

If you aren't sure what resonates with you at the moment, taking time out to reflect can help. Tuning in to your inner guidance can provide valuable information.

One technique is to think about something that you have enjoyed and has provided a meaningful spiritual experience. Let yourself fully engage in this visualization. What was the activity? Who was present? What were you doing? What was your part? Were you an active participant? Were you leading the event? Or were you there as an attendee? Tune in to your feelings about this activity. How does your body feel as you put yourself back in this event? What parts of your body feel good or relaxed? Is your heart happy?

Now, contrast this with an activity or event that you did not enjoy. Again, what was the event? Were you an active participant? Were you the leader? Were you there as an attendee? What are you feeling in your body as you tune in to this activity? How are you feeling in your gut area? Do you feel tense or unhappy?

If you can identify where in your body you have feelings about activities you enjoy versus those that you don't, you have a great tool to assist you in determining your next step. For some of you, this may be a familiar process, and for others, it may be new. You may have been raised in an environment, as I was, where you were taught to hide your feelings, and now you are learning to tune in and acknowledge them as a guide for what you want and who you truly are. The more you practice listening to your feelings, the easier it will be. Then you will have a ready tool to help you in your decision-making process.

In the past, I often made decisions based on a mental level. I reasoned out what the rational course of action would be. Even though my heart was urging me to make a different decision, I reverted to doing what most "rational" and "logical" people would do. When I did this, even though the action would turn out okay, my heart would be yearning for the course of action I didn't take. I would be thinking, "What if I had only taken the action I really wanted to take?"

I decided to test this out on a spiritual pilgrimage to Peru. On a pilgrimage where bus travel is involved, each person is usually limited to one large suitcase and a backpack so that all luggage can be accommodated.

On this occasion, many of the other fellow pilgrims were opting for backpacks. Although I had a nice backpack that I had used on other pilgrimages, my heart kept crying out for me to take a cross-body tote bag that I really liked and had taken on many other trips to places such as Greece and Canada. It would be accessible whenever I needed anything, and it would hold almost as much as my backpack. It also felt like an old friend. I wrestled with the decision for many days. After all, being a Libra, as I am, making decisions isn't always easy, even for such a seemingly small one.

I went back and forth as to which bag to take. After

much deliberation, I decided to test each option and see how I felt. When I held the backpack, I felt a tenseness in my solar plexus and an overall tightness in my body. When I held the tote bag, I felt a lightness in my heart and an overall relaxed feeling in my body. I knew that those were my physical signals for what made my heart sing. A tense feeling in my solar plexus and overall body tightness was a no, and a light feeling in my heart and overall relaxed body feeling was a yes.

So, I opted for the tote bag. As soon as I made this decision, my heart soared. It felt like me. I knew that I would be happy with it, and it met all of my needs for a small bag on the pilgrimage.

After I made this decision, other decisions around the pilgrimage seemed to flow more easily.

I decided to take a hot pink journal instead of the red one that I normally would have taken. Each time I tried to pack the red journal, something didn't feel right. Finally, once again I listened to what made my heart sing, and I took the pink journal and was very happy with my decision.

By being true to myself on such seemingly small decisions, I opened the floodgates for larger ones to flow.

I realized that for so long I had made decisions based on what I thought other people expected rather than what I wanted to do. Now it was time for me to do what made my heart sing.

What I learned is that we need to take as much time as necessary in deciding what we want. Many seasoned spiritual travelers are taking a sabbatical to assess where they have been and what they want next. This is not selfish. It is honoring yourself as a unique individual and honoring the path you are on. It is acknowledging that you are a serious spiritual Being and that you want to make your next step one that truly honors who you are and is in alignment with your spiritual mission.

Even making a decision about a small part of your next step can open the door to a larger step on your path.

Making decisions and being true to yourself could be compared to developing a muscle. If you have not been accustomed to doing what makes your heart sing and have only been thinking about what others want, being true to yourself is a new skill. It is like developing any other skill such as learning a new computer program or increasing physical stamina. The more you exercise and develop this new skill, the more proficient you will become and the easier it will be. Soon, you will be a master at making decisions.

◆ ◆ ◆

Let Your Heart Sing

~ Inspiration from The Angelic Realm ~

Beloved Ones,

The heart is where you begin to access the energy of the higher dimensions. The energy of the heart is the energy of Love. The energy of the higher dimensions is based on Love. This is a universal Love that goes far beyond romantic love.

The energy of Love is a universal vibration that encompasses all of Creation. It is an energy that hums throughout the Universe and connects both the manifested and unmanifested potential of All That Is. It is the substance of pure Light.

The Light connects you with All That Is through the Divine Spark in your heart center. This is the place where you can turn to feel your connection with all of humanity and All That Is.

When you live in such a way that your heart sings, the energy in your heart center remains clear, and your Light shines brightly. The clearer the energy in your heart center is, the more brightly your Light will shine.

When your heart sings, the Light is coherent and moving in the same direction in an organized manner. There is no push or pull directing the energy to move in divergent directions. You are clear about what you want and what makes your heart sing. This allows the energy to move forward in an organized way.

When this occurs, your personal energetic frequency is higher. This allows you to access the energy in the higher dimensions, and you begin to rise to higher levels. There is no struggle or strain. It happens automatically because you have allowed your heart to sing.

The many planetary energy shifts are aiding the process of allowing your heart to sing. Each shift is bringing things to the surface and to your awareness for examination. You have the opportunity to decide what makes your heart sing.

When you are clear about what makes your heart sing, you are being offered the opportunity to move to higher levels.

Being clear about what makes your heart sing is an ongoing process. As a Being of Light, your energy field is constantly changing and flowing according to your thoughts and emotions, as well as to the planetary energy shifts. This provides a wonderful opportunity for you to move forward.

Being aware of the changing energy is an important part of letting your heart sing. This allows you to move and flow with the energy. It allows you to let go of what no longer feels right for you. This frees up energy for you to explore new interests. When this occurs, your energy is constantly renewing itself, and your heart sings.

Each day brings the possibility of new insights because you are living in the moment. You become aware of the concept that the present moment is all that is. When you are aware of the present moment, a feeling of peacefulness begins to flow from you, and your heart sings.

As you focus on whatever makes your heart sing, this allows the insights to flow more naturally because you have raised your energetic vibration. You are in that space of coherent Light. You are in the flow. The more you engage in this process, the more it will occur. Soon, it will become a way of living for you.

This does not mean that you abandon all responsibilities. It means that you consciously make time each day for doing what makes your heart sing. These activities that make your heart sing begin to build a bridge or a network of points of Light that carry you throughout whatever you need to do during your day.

The more points of Light you create, the more easily your day will flow. You begin to rise to a higher vibration that sustains you as you move forward. It is a creating of points of Light and maintaining them by being aware of what makes your heart sing.

If you find an activity that previously made you happy and it no longer calls to you, bless it for the happiness it brought you and release it with Love to the Universe. The peaceful energy that surrounded this activity is then free to transmute and transform into something that will be an energetic fit for you at the current time.

When you remain in the present moment, you are more aware of when these shifts occur. You are able to make changes gradually and more easily. It becomes a flow of being aware of what makes your heart sing at the present moment.

As this process occurs, your heart sings, and you begin to flow with the music of the spheres.

Know that you are greatly loved.

~ The Angelic Realm

The Flow of Being True to Yourself

—⋉⋊—

You have determined how to know what makes your heart sing. You know you want to make a change, but you're still not sure it is worth the effort it will take.

You still may be asking yourself why you need to think about being true to yourself at this time when you have conformed to the expectations of others for so long, or because you are already well-established on your spiritual path. Sometimes, changing may seem daunting and like too much effort. You still may be asking yourself if it really matters.

The night often seems darkest just before the dawn. This sometimes can be a sign that you are on the verge of moving to a higher dimensional level, and the extra energy you apply at this point can lift you to your next stage of advancement.

One way to overcome this feeling of uncertainty is to examine each area of your life.

There is a growing recognition in many circles that one size doesn't fit all. This ranges from types of exercise to diet to clothes to hobbies to careers to spiritual paths.

You are composed of body, mind, and spirit. Each component is made of energy. When the components are in alignment, you move forward in a peaceful and harmonious manner. However, if one part is out of alignment, your entire being feels off-kilter. You are not being true to yourself in that particular area.

For example, in the physical body, you may try to eat foods that are the current fad. You put on a good face when you are with friends and pretend that you like what the latest trend is saying you should eat. However, your body begins to rebel and you find yourself not functioning at an optimal level. The same thing may occur with exercise. You know what makes you feel good, but the current craze is to do a different type of exercise. You try it, but you feel miserable. You may even experience an injury if you continue. Your body is giving you signals that this is not for you, but you haven't listened. When your physical body isn't feeling harmonious, it is hard to experience mental well-being, much less focus on your spiritual path.

On the mental level, an example would be the

types of books you read or programs you watch on television. Your friends may rave about what they are reading and watching, and you decide that you need to do the same in order to fit in and be able to carry on a good conversation. However, you feel a sense of dread whenever you pick up the book you think you need to read, and your nerves feel jangled after you watch a television program you don't enjoy. The end result is that you feel irritated because you haven't done what you really wanted to do. What you selected was not an energetic fit for you. Your body reflects this, and it is hard to feel spiritual.

My personal experience on the mental level was that I bought many spiritual and self-help books. If someone mentioned a book they had enjoyed, I immediately went to the bookstore to get a copy. Often, when I started to read it, I didn't really enjoy it and couldn't get involved with the message it contained. One day I looked at a large stack of books and realized that I was never going to read them, so I packed them up and donated them. When I dropped them off at the donation point, I immediately felt free. I had released a large amount of pent-up mental energy that was bound up in being someone other than who I was.

On the spiritual level, you may be following the

path in which you were raised, the path that you think society expects you to follow, or the current trend, but you are miserable. After going to a spiritual gathering or a service, you may feel disconnected and ask yourself why you went. Your mind floats to a type of spiritual experience that you could have done instead that would have left you feeling fulfilled.

As I discussed in my first book, I have experienced many religious and spiritual traditions along the way. Each path had some parts that I enjoyed, but I didn't want to give up the practices in other traditions that were meaningful to me. Finally, I realized that a personal spiritual path would allow me to embrace the practices from each path that called to me, and I felt a sense of peace and fulfillment.

When you are not true to yourself in one of these areas, your motivation to be true to yourself in another area is compromised. Soon you realize that you are off-track and need to make some corrections.

Periodically I like to assess where I am in each area of my life. For several years I have used a process where I write down my ideal state of being for each area such as physical well-being, spirituality, family, friends, career, and finances.

Before I begin this process, I go into a period of silence. It may be a few moments or longer, depending on how my schedule has been. I wait until I feel centered. I tune in to my heart center, and I ask the Higher Beings to join me.

Then I reflect on each area of my life and what would make my heart sing at that current point on my path.

Next, I write positive statements beginning with "I am" or "I have" for each area. Usually I have several statements under each area. I always add the phrase "this or something better" to each area and express gratitude for what I have received.

Then I tune in to my body to see how I feel and whether each statement makes my heart sing. If I find that my heart doesn't sing with a particular statement, I have the power to change what I have written.

I review it often to see whether I want to make any adjustments. Because I keep this on my computer, making a change in the document is easy. Whenever I feel a need to revise something, adjusting the document is a simple process.

Over the years I discovered that some of what I had written down was what I thought others expected me to do rather than what made my heart sing. So, I deleted those items. I only kept what felt like me.

I found that when I made a change in one area, I was motivated to be true to myself in other areas. Each area flowed seamlessly into the next. The more I embraced being true to myself in one area, the more I wanted to change things in other areas. My energy began to flow from the outer to the inner and back out again with each change.

It is easier to progress spiritually when we are in alignment and are being true to ourselves.

We cannot hide our feelings in the higher dimensions because our energy field and vibration are how we are known and recognized at that level.

Your energy field will be clear and sparkling when you are being true to yourself on all levels. If what you are communicating to others matches the way you really feel, everything is aligned, and your energy field is clear. However, if you are attempting to communicate one thing to others while you are trying to hide your true feelings, your energy field will appear cloudy or muddy, and your beautiful Light cannot shine brightly. You want your energy to radiate the sparkling jewel of Light that you are.

You are being true to yourself when your words and your actions match your feelings.

❖ ❖ ❖

The Time is Now to Be True to Yourself

~ Inspiration from The Angelic Realm ~

Beloved Ones,

You may be asking yourself why being true to yourself is more important now than it has been previously. You may be thinking that this is something you can put off until tomorrow, next month, or next year.

It is because of the increasing urgency and speed with which the ascension process is taking place that it is of the utmost importance that you be true to yourself. This impacts both your own ascension as well as that of humanity and the planet. Because All Is One, your thread of energy impacts everything around you in the seen and the unseen. You have a great opportunity to help advance the ascension of everyone and everything.

First, examine and assess where you are. Being true to yourself is very important during the ascension process, for you must unify your energy field so that all of the cells are moving together harmoniously in the same direction. This is a basic energetic principle to help you advance and ascend. A house divided cannot stand.

This same principle can be applied when thinking about ascension. If your energy is pulled in several different and sometimes opposing directions, it cannot move forward in a harmonious manner. The reverse principle also applies. When a house is unified, it is a fortress that withstands all elements that may come. When all of your energy is unified and directed toward a specific path, you can make rapid progress because there is no dissension and no doubt as to whether to take a certain path.

As a group, humanity has come through a time where choices were being made. Many avenues and paths were being explored. It was a time of great experimentation to determine which path was the right fit for each person. It was easier to change from path to path because the energy was moving at a slower pace, and the change was energetically easier on the energy field of the individual.

For a long time, the energy moved at a slower pace to allow you to explore and determine the best fit for you. There were many paths from which to choose, and it was important for you to experience the variety in order to make the right selection for yourself. In the ascension process there is no exclusive path. There are many avenues to ascension. Each one leads to the same goal of reunification with Source.

The important part is to honor the path you have chosen. It brings about a sense of harmony throughout your entire Being when you are true to yourself and your innermost yearnings for ascension.

Being true to yourself first involves being honest with yourself about what is really important to you. This is a process that needs to feel right to you. As you focus on your chosen path and what it involves, pay attention to how it feels. Notice how each part of your body feels as you imagine yourself on your path. Spend a few moments reflecting on each chakra and whether your path resonates harmoniously with it. If you have hesitation at any point, explore what that hesitation is. It may be a signal that a minor adjustment is needed. It may call you to explore some of your long-held beliefs.

This is a time of purification and releasing any old

beliefs and patterns that you no longer wish to carry forward. It may also be a signal for you to make a slight adjustment in your path in order to be true to the core values that you wish to carry forward. Whatever the case, it is important for the energy to be clear and for any issues to be resolved. You may wish to call upon the Violet Flame to assist you in transmuting and transforming those things that you are ready to release.

When you have cleared the energy, you are ready to move forward. When your path and each aspect resonate harmoniously with each chakra, all of your energy systems are working together. This allows you to move forward with ease and grace.

This is an ongoing process, for as you continue to move forward on your path, you will be given many choice points to affirm and confirm whether a certain step is consistent with your path. It is important at each point to decide whether that step resonates with you. You always have free will, and moving forward with a clarity of energy is essential for your next step. Resolving conflicts within your energy field as they arise will be much easier than pushing them aside and waiting until a later time to examine what the discomfort and uncertainty are about.

When you are clear about your current point along your path, it is important for your thoughts, words, and actions to be consistent with what you have chosen. This can be a point of choice of direction. It may involve changing patterns that previously held attraction for you, or it may involve establishing new patterns. You may explore different options to see which one feels right for you and is congruent with your chosen path.

For example, if you have decided that having a daily period of quiet time for yourself for reflection, meditation, and study will help you to advance spiritually and you do not honor this commitment to yourself, it will set up a discordant pattern of energy within you because you have not matched your actions with your intentions. This is where you have an opportunity to make an adjustment so that your intentions and actions will flow energetically in the same direction. It is far better energetically to take small steps that are congruent with your intentions than to plan large steps that you know you will not honor because this sets up an imbalance of energy.

This is different from setting a spiritual ideal toward which to move. When you have a desired goal of moving along your ascension path, this is a larger goal. The small steps are the smaller goals along the way. When you achieve a small goal of making your actions congruent with your intentions, you have progressed on the path of ascension. This is a harmonious energetic flow because all of your energy is moving in the same direction.

When your energy is moving harmoniously, you radiate a sense of peace and calmness to those around you. This point of stillness begins at your core. You have resolved all concerns around that part of your path.

At certain times the steps you are taking may be very different than the path of those around you. This can be a time to exercise discernment. It does not mean abandoning your own values and path. It does mean honoring the free will of those around you. It may mean knowing when to speak your truth and when to be silent. It means speaking your truth with Love and acceptance for all, even when they do not agree with your choice of path. Your Love and acceptance of them does not negate your own path. It is simply honoring them and their choice while remaining true to yourself.

Set aside a time for a daily review to focus on your

path and to assess how well your words and actions adhered to it. Also, review whether you showed respect for the paths of others. Making small adjustments regularly is much easier than realizing that you have veered off the path that you set for yourself and then having to make a bigger correction.

Keep the Love of all and the desire for greatest good uppermost in your mind as you focus on your highest good and being true to yourself. Remember that Universal Love is a unifying energy. A harmonious co-existence of all paths can lead to much peace for humanity as well as for each individual. This peace and harmony will ripple out into the Universe and all of Creation for highest good.

Know that you are greatly loved.

~ The Angelic Realm

PART 2

CREATING THE PATH

OF

YOUR HEART'S DESIRE

Creating from a Multidimensional Perspective

—⋘⋙—

You have identified what makes your heart sing and what you want each part of your life to look like. Before you move forward, there is another component to consider as you create the path your heart desires. That factor is multidimensionality.

As a seasoned traveler on the spiritual path, you are already aware of the steps in co-creation and manifestation. You know that you need to set a clear intention, tune in to receive ideas and guidance, and take action steps to bring your dreams into reality.

But have you considered that each part of this process is a piece of a larger mosaic? Your path forms a unique pattern as you shape each step of your journey into a design. You may even receive new steps to add to your path as your awareness increases.

In creating an actual physical mosaic, you have an

idea for your design. Pieces may be placed in whatever order you desire until they form the picture you have visualized.

In looking at co-creation from a multidimensional perspective, a similar process occurs. Each part is a necessary step, but the process may vary. You may even receive new steps to add to your path as your awareness increases.

By looking at your path as a spiritual mosaic, you develop a multidimensional approach. The parts are there, but they do not necessarily follow a linear direction. That is the third-dimensional way. In the multiple dimensions, everything is occurring at the same time.

Your path no longer has to follow a linear sequence. Let it flow as it unfolds. When you do this, you are following your authentic Self. The steps you would follow in a linear sequence may occur in a seemingly random fashion in a multidimensional approach, or they may fold seamlessly into each other.

Know that all is in Divine Order. Let your intuition guide you. If you feel prompted to work on a step of co-creation that seems out of order, there may be a reason. You may learn about an opportunity that will fit nicely with your desired path, or you may meet someone who can help you with a particular aspect of it.

You also have flexibility when you view your path as a mosaic.

When one piece no longer fits with the overall design, it can be replaced with one that reflects where you are at the present moment. Or you may decide to create an entirely new design.

In this section, we will highlight various aspects of the mosaic that occur in making your dreams a reality.

Setting a Clear Intention

———⚭———

So now what? You have identified your special gifts and abilities, you have learned how to identify what makes your heart sing, you have written down what you want in each area of your life, and you have looked at things from a multidimensional perspective.

This is valuable data, but you still may be wondering how you want to shape it into the next meaningful part of your path.

Even a seasoned spiritual traveler asks these questions along the way. Remember, at each new vibrational level, the steps, processes, and lessons will repeat, but you will be viewing them from a higher perspective and shaping this data at a higher vibrational level.

So, what is your next step?

Are you clear with your intention? As a seasoned spiritual traveler, you are well aware of the need to set a clear intention as part of manifesting your heart's desire for your path. It may even seem like a well-worn cliché to talk about this, but it is an important step to take, especially in the new, higher vibrational energy. Spending time on this part of the process can help you harness this energy and call in the assistance of the Higher Realms.

You may have an idea of your intention for the next step on your path, or it still may be vague. Sometimes when you are moving to a higher level, it can feel like starting a new course of study. And perhaps it is, for you are evolving into an even more powerful Being of Light. The concepts of spiritual laws become more refined at the higher levels or dimensions.

Each part of co-creation takes on a more dynamic or multifaceted approach at a higher level. There are subtleties and nuances to consider. The slightest doubt about an intention can be magnified at a higher frequency, so clarity is extremely important. If you feel yourself having even the slightest doubt about your stated intention, this is the time to stop and examine where that is coming from. You may need to go back and examine each part of your intention and make adjustments as needed. At the higher dimensions, thoughts, feelings, words, and intentions manifest much faster, and sending mixed signals could create a jumbled or even chaotic outcome. Remember that everything is vibration, and intentions need to carry a similar, harmonious vibration for a favorable outcome.

Therefore, having a clear intention can assist you in moving along your path with a sense of ease.

Perhaps you want to have a clearer understanding of spiritual concepts, you may want to manifest a particular project, or you may want to scale back your outer activities to spend more time going inward. Whatever you desire, having a clear intention can help you draw the Beings of Light into your awareness to assist you.

A clear intention defines the end point or goal of your current desire or project and is stated in the present tense as if it has already manifested. It begins with "I am ... " or "I have ..." or similar words. This process is important in a time where many energies compete for your attention. A clear intention leads to focused attention, and you move forward more easily.

Setting a clear intention is an energetic principle that harnesses the vibratory forces around you.

The Universal Law of Attraction states that like attracts like. The Law of Vibration states that everything vibrates. Your intention carries a vibration, and a clearly stated intention attracts circumstances of a similar vibration.

Therefore, the extra time spent on this step can help you move forward and achieve the desired results on your path.

I have had my own learning experiences with setting a clear intention. In the past, I have sometimes skipped the step of setting a clear intention, and later I realized my mistake in not doing this important part.

For many years I have struggled with what I thought others expected me to do versus doing something that made my heart sing. Sometimes I didn't know what that was. I just knew that I was ready for a change from what I had been doing, especially when it meant exploring new realms. Setting a clear intention was just another case of needing to be true to myself.

I had one experience that highlighted this dilemma very clearly for me.

Very often I have tried to balance the competing forces of what I felt society expected me to do versus reaching out to a different calling or refinement on my spiritual path.

One such instance occurred after I was ordained as a non-denominational minister. I loved the choice I had made to select this as part of my path, and I enjoyed performing the traditional ceremonies such as marriages and celebrations of life. So, I decided to take additional training that could prepare me to further my skills and abilities as an ordained minister. I was excited because I felt that this would open additional opportunities for me to be of greater service in traditional ministerial roles such as speaking to organized religious groups.

I embarked on my course of study and made steady progress. I knew in my heart that this would help me in my desire to gain additional credentials and to be of greater service.

Then one day I felt that I was being called to a slightly different way to be of service in a ministerial role. It manifested as an inner feeling that something was not yet complete for me. There seemed to be a missing component in my Being. I was still searching for that piece that would propel me to my next step. I felt very conflicted because I wanted the additional training and credentials, but my Higher Self was telling me that I was to pursue something different.

Then seemingly all at once, an opportunity landed

in my lap to study and teach a less traditional course of spiritual study. As I thought about this new possibility, my heart soared. Not only would I be studying with the Higher Beings, but I would also be able to share this knowledge with others and inspire them on their path.

It was a classic example of deciding between what felt safe and enjoyable versus expanding into other areas that were further removed from the mainstream. What would people think?

I had set my original intention at a mental level, but my feelings at a heart level were pulling me in a different direction. I realized that it would be hard for me to pursue my original goal of gaining additional training in a traditional area when my heart was going in a different direction. My thoughts and feelings were not congruent, and I was sending mixed messages to the Universe. The water was muddy. I did not have a clear intention.

Finally, I knew I had to do what was calling to me at a heart level. I pursued the less traditional course of study of angelic wisdom teachings and esoteric knowledge and began teaching this material to small groups. I loved it! I was getting to do what I loved, and I was providing the participants with an opportunity for expanded spiritual growth.

At last I had a clear intention. In my mind I could clearly state my intention, and this was backed up with feelings at a heart level. I could move forward in a clear way. All of the energy was congruent and focused on a clear intention.

I could be true to myself in what I was doing.

As we move forward with setting our intentions, we may want to pause occasionally to see whether our stated intentions resonate with us both at a feeling and at a mental level. If anything about it feels off, then we can examine it more closely and make adjustments as needed.

This allows us to remain true to ourselves where we are at the present moment.

❖ ❖ ❖

The Light of Focused Intention

~ Inspiration from The Angelic Realm ~

Beloved Ones,

The Light of focused intention can help you move forward on your spiritual path.

You are living in a time of great opportunity. Much new and higher vibrational energy is arriving on your planet, and you are in control of the way in which you wish to shape this energy to meet your goals and state of being as you progress on your spiritual path.

There is no right or wrong way in which you should shape it. It is totally your choice as to how you use this energy. The important thing is to be clear about how you want to use it and what you want the outcome to be.

There are several points to consider when thinking about the new energy. It arrives in a neutral form. There are no predetermined outcomes. It has the high potential to manifest in whatever configuration you desire. Because it is of a higher quality and the energy is moving much more quickly, the manifestation will occur more rapidly than it has previously. Therefore, it is very important to be clear about what you want.

It is no longer helpful to dwell on things that could be less than positive for yourself or others. Wherever you place your thoughts will begin to shape the energy into the form of your thoughts, especially if they are accompanied by strong emotions. Remaining positive is helpful.

Therefore, the first step is to be clear about what you wish to manifest. This is setting a clear intention.

There are many areas from which to choose. You can think about aspects such as your physical being, family, friends, career, spiritual path, or any other area that is important to you. There may be one area that leaps out to you for attention as you begin this process.

For example, you may decide that you want to focus on your spiritual path. You may be considering adding a new spiritual practice, or you may be reviewing what you are currently doing to see if it fits who you are at this time. Remember that you are constantly evolving, and it is important that whatever you select in any area needs to feel right for you at this time on your path.

In the review process, you may wish to consider different options. This could be compared to brainstorming. As you consider an option, see how it feels to you as you picture yourself doing it. Does it lift you up and make you want to embrace it? Or, does it fill you with a sense of dread? The way you feel when you picture yourself in this practice will give you a clue as to whether you want to add it, or if it is already what you do, it will help you decide whether to keep it.

You may wish to consider an additional area, or you may decide to focus just on one for the moment.

Once you have decided what you want to manifest, state your intention clearly. Get a focused picture in your mind of yourself in the situation.

For example, if you want to set a time for meditation, state clearly to yourself that, "I am meditating daily," or whatever words you want to add. Picture yourself selecting a time of day that works best for you. See yourself sitting in a quiet and calm spot that will invite you to meditate. Picture yourself feeling relaxed and happy as you enjoy your meditation time. See yourself at the end of your meditation feeling fulfilled spiritually from your time in quiet communion.

This is setting your intention and focus for the practice. The more you can picture or imagine yourself actually doing this, the stronger the intention and focus will be.

When you add emotions and feelings to your visualization, it becomes even stronger and more powerful. Your intention to set a time for meditation becomes fixed in your mind. The more you focus on it, the stronger it becomes.

As you begin to add actions to your intention, it increases the strength even more. If your intention is to meditate, each time you sit in your meditation spot and actually meditate, the energy builds and the focus on your intention increases.

You have gone through a cycle of setting your intention and adding focus. You have reviewed the possibilities to consider and selected the one that feels most like you. You have stated your intention clearly. You have pictured yourself taking the action and feeling the rewards of having done so. Then you have actually taken the action, and this has reinforced your intention.

It is important to continue to put your intention into practice until it becomes a habit. The more you do this, the stronger it will become. You will have applied the Light and power of setting an intention and strengthening it with focus and resolve.

As you are continuing to apply the Light and putting your intention into practice, ask for the highest and best good for all concerned.

We are with you as you set a clear intention for your path.

Know that you are greatly loved.

~ The Angelic Realm

Putting Your Intentions into Motion

—————∽⟨⟩∾—————

Have you ever wished that you could wave a magic wand and manifest your dreams?

We have all probably felt that way at one time or another, even though we know that is not likely to happen.

As seasoned travelers on the spiritual path, we know that action needs to follow setting an intention or a goal.

At earlier stages of our path, we may have encountered persons who thought that once an intention was stated, it would automatically manifest without further effort. As we began to explore the manifestation process, we realized that action needs to follow intentions.

In reality, we are co-creators with the Universe.

With our understanding that we are now capable of multidimensional participation, we are even more aware of the need to do our part after we have tuned in to the Higher Realms for assistance with creating the path of our heart's desire.

In a multidimensional process, as in a third-dimensional one, taking action is necessary. When we receive an idea, we can evaluate it for its relevance to our stated intention. Then we can determine its feasibility. These are all important parts of the process of manifestation. If we get a green light on the answers to these questions, then we can proceed on taking action.

Sometimes despite our best efforts, we may find that our stated intention is not coming into reality.

We may even ask ourselves, "If I am so spiritual, why aren't my dreams manifesting?"

Does it seem that everyone else's dreams are manifesting while you are left on the sidelines?

Having a goal and not seeing it come to fruition can be very frustrating and disappointing. It may even cause you to question whether you are on the right spiritual path.

When thoughts such as these arise, reviewing the process of manifestation can help you identify where things have gone awry and how you can make adjustments to move forward.

Manifesting begins with a clear idea of what you want. You spend time considering possibilities, daydreaming about them and how they would feel, and brainstorming ideas about steps to take to make them a reality.

After this initial process has occurred, you have condensed your idea down to a goal. Having a clear statement allows you to be sure in your own Being that this is what you want. Your thoughts and feelings need to be congruent in your goal statement. If you aren't completely sure that your desired goal is what you want, it may show up as a feeling of unease in the solar plexus or other area of your physical body. Or you may have a nagging feeling that something just isn't right.

If you ignore these signals, they may show up later when your goal doesn't manifest as you had desired.

The old adage to "be careful what you wish for" may come to mind.

One possibility to consider is where you are on your spiritual journey. You have achieved great strides in your ascension process, and you are now working at a multidimensional level. You can see things from a higher perspective as your awareness is expanding.

As you progress, your goals may take on a different level of vibration.

Perhaps you have stated your goal at a third-dimensional level when your heart is calling you to work at a multidimensional level. The type of goal is the same, but it is a difference of degree. It could be compared to viewing things standing in the middle of a crowd as opposed to viewing the situation floating above the crowd. Your stated intention may have a completely different perspective when you view it from a multidimensional level.

After putting out a clear statement of intention and matching it to your current level of multidimensionality, the next step is taking action. Dreams do not automatically manifest just because you have set the goal and put it out to the Universe. Action steps are needed.

Of course, the Higher Beings are there to help you if you ask them. Because the Earth is a free-will planet, the Higher Beings are not allowed to work with you unless you ask for their help. When you do ask, they are happy to be there to assist you. It could be considered a working partnership.

They may bring ideas, "chance" meetings with others, or circumstances that magically appear.

When these occurrences happen, the next step is to do your part by taking action. This is the place that trips up those who have forgotten that taking action is a crucial part of manifestation.

When you have set a clear intention that is aligned with your thoughts and feelings, you have asked for assistance, and you have taken the action steps, you are on the road to manifesting your goal.

❖ ❖ ❖

Conscious Co-Creation

~ Inspiration from The Angelic Realm ~

Beloved Ones,

You are advancing rapidly on your ascension path. You have expanded your consciousness, and you are aware that you are now functioning on a multidimensional level. You are able to view situations from a third-dimensional perspective and then zoom out to see them from a much larger vantage point.

Because you are functioning at this level, you are

now co-creating at a multidimensional level.

You may be finding that your thoughts and desires manifest much more rapidly than they did previously. This is because you are working with higher frequencies of refined Light. These are the building blocks of your creations. When you focus on what you want and add the actions necessary, your dreams become a reality.

This is why we would like to impress on you the importance of realizing that you are a conscious co-creator at a multidimensional level.

As such, the steps of manifestation that you have mastered at lower dimensional levels take on an even greater impact at the higher levels. Therefore, it can be helpful to review the importance of each step.

Your thoughts and intentions are very powerful, especially when amplified by emotions and strong desires.

When you are brainstorming ideas for what you would like and how you want to design the next step of your path, remaining objective in the beginning of this process will allow you to generate ideas without becoming too strongly attached to them. You will not accidentally set wheels into motion for manifesting an idea before you are ready to commit to it.

As you review your ideas, consider each one and determine whether it makes your heart sing. If it does, then think about whether it is practical and is something you would like to manifest.

After you have selected your desired next step, then you can formulate it into an intention. Make sure you have stated it in a positive way as if it has already manifested. Remember to be sure that your goal is for the highest and best good of all concerned.

Then focus on how you will feel when your goal has come into fruition. Focusing on the statement you have written and adding the emotional fuel sets the stage for taking action. The stronger the focus, the greater energy it will have. You have sent your intentions to the Universe.

When you send your desires out in this way, the higher particles of Light are attracted to form the object of your desires. This can only occur when the goal is for highest good.

It is likely that you will begin to receive ideas for action steps to carry out for manifesting your goal.

Taking the necessary action is important because you are in a co-creative role. Your desired goal will not manifest simply because you have written it down on paper or drawn a picture of it. Taking action is crucial.

The Higher Beings of Light will assist you if you call on them and if your creation is for highest good. They may bring pieces of information to your attention through a book, an article, or something you hear on television. They may also arrange for you to see someone who can help you with your project. When they do their part by bringing the ideas, you carry out your part by taking the necessary action. Therefore, the co-creative partnership functions as a gentle and dynamic flow between you.

The more you take an active role in this process, the more cooperation you will experience with the Higher Realms. Through your focused attention on your goals and the action steps you take, you are likely to find that your goals manifest more smoothly.

If you reach a point where your project is not moving as you had planned, you may wish to review the goal to see if it is still what makes your heart sing, whether it is feasible, and whether it is for highest good. Then you can make adjustments if needed.

By moving forward in this manner, you are a conscious co-creator with the Beings of Light.

Beloveds, we are happy to work with you on your glorious projects of co-creation.

Know that you are greatly loved.

~ The Angelic Realm

Working with the Higher Beings

—❊❊—

Setting a clear intention is an important part of co-creating your next step with the Beings of Light in the Higher Realms.

As you know, Earth is a free-will planet. As such, the Higher Beings are not allowed to interfere with your path or decisions unless you ask for their help. As much as they want to guide us, it is necessary to ask for their help for them to assist.

There are many Beings in all areas of the Higher Realms waiting to assist us. These include the Angelic Realm, the Ascended Masters, and many others.

In the Higher Realms there is no competition. Each Being has its own particular area of expertise, and teamwork is the norm. You do not have to worry about offending a particular Being that you usually work with if you decide to work with another one on a particular project.

I have found that whenever I have begun working on a particular area of study or a project, if I have called on the Higher Realms, I am immediately connected with a Higher Being who specializes in just what I need. Of course, my regular guides and teachers are also there. It has been a great comfort to me to continue to call on these special assistants over the years for help in their area of specialty.

One specific example happened for me when I was required to take two additional graduate courses as part of my job. Although I was excited about learning new information, it had been ten years since I had completed my formal graduate degree program, and the thought of going back to school was daunting. Would I be able to keep up? Could I do the required projects? How would I do on the exams? Because my employer was paying for the courses, I felt even more pressure to succeed.

As I was pondering how to proceed, I decided to ask for a guide for each course. I was fortunate that the two courses were being taught in consecutive semesters so that I could place all of my attention on one course at a time.

Before the first course began, I went into meditation and thought about the course title and the content involved. I had a clear picture of what was required. I set an intention to be able to understand the concepts involved and know how to apply them. I also wanted to make an A in the course, even though I was taking it on a pass/fail basis. I asked the Universe to send me a guide that would be a perfect match for me and what I needed in that course. Very soon, an elegant gentleman dressed in a tuxedo and working at a desk appeared in my mind's eye. He introduced himself and said that he would be working with me on the course. He told me that he was very knowledgeable and successful in his field of work. He had an air of confidence that he instilled in me, and he told me that I would be just fine. And he was right!

Each time I went to class or sat down to study, I pictured him and called his name, and he appeared. I felt a sense of confidence that I was not facing the study alone. True to his word, he helped me every step of the way.

I understood the concepts involved in the course and completed my projects on time. And I received an A in the course! I was elated!

I had proved to myself that if I set a clear intention, I would receive the help I requested. Of course, I always expressed my gratitude after each time my guide worked with me.

Soon, it was time for me to begin the second course of study.

I sat down and repeated the same process I had used in the first course. I thought about the course title and what I would need to learn and accomplish. It felt very daunting because there would be a lot of science involved. Still, I forged ahead.

I went into meditation and stated my intention to learn the concepts and apply them successfully, along with making an A in the course even though I was taking it on a pass/fail basis. I asked for someone to help me with this course. I knew it would be a different guide than the one in the first course because I needed someone with the particular expertise in this area of study. Almost immediately, a lady in a white lab coat appeared in my mind's eye. She was in a scientific laboratory setting. She told me her name and said she would be working with me in that course of study.

I followed the same steps I had used in the first course. Whenever I sat down to study, work on a project, or take an exam, I pictured her in my mind, called her name, and asked her to work with me. Again, I had great success in that course. I even got an

A, and I was thrilled!

I thanked her and the Universe for assisting me in this course.

As I was reflecting on what had happened with each course, I had a great appreciation for the process of clearly stating my intention and asking for the appropriate help. I felt that I had received the perfect guides to assist me because I had so clearly stated what I needed and asked for the specific help involved.

As an added bonus, these guides have remained with me since that time whenever I am working with anything in their field of expertise. I repeat the same process I used in the courses. I picture them, call their names, and state the name of the project on which I am working and the type of help I need. They always come through for me, and I feel very comforted knowing that they are there and are willing to help.

An additional benefit in working with the Higher Beings is that our own vibration is raised when we attune to them. Each time we think about or call on these Beings, we are connecting with their energy. The more we work with them as co-creators, the more our own Energetic Signature increases, and we continue to rise higher in the multidimensions.

◆ ◆ ◆

A Partnership with the Higher Beings

~ Inspiration from The Angelic Realm ~

Beloved Ones,

You are in a partnership with the Higher Beings. As you move forward on your ascension path, we are working with you even more closely. Our partnership could be considered as one between the seen and the unseen realms. We are happy to work with you whenever you call on us.

Our work with you can proceed more smoothly when you have a clear intention about what you would like our partnership to include.

The importance of having a clear intention is that this is what we, in the Higher Realms, will use to assist you when you call on us. At the levels of the Higher Dimensions your intentions will manifest almost instantaneously. Therefore, you want to be sure that what you are manifesting is of the highest and purest vibration.

As you know, you will experience your manifestations as energy returning to you. Energy travels in a circle, and so whatever you send out will return to you in like kind. Manifesting a very pure intent at this level will affect not only you but many others in all dimensions. Therefore, the ramifications of what you think, what you do, and any other actions that result from it, will have a much greater impact. It is not only you who will reap the actions you bring forth, it will be many multitudes. It will also affect others in the multidimensions.

There is great responsibility the further that you move up the ascension path. This is why we give you the opportunity to move at your own pace as you work with us. When you move at your own pace, it gives you an opportunity to examine each situation that you create and see whether it was beneficial for you, for others, and for the greatest good of all. If you find that there were glitches in any part, you can go back and see what you would have done differently if you had thought about those possibilities in the beginning. By doing this at lower levels, you have an opportunity to learn and practice when the stakes are not as great as they are in the Higher Dimensions.

This is very similar to the way a child learns. When you give them opportunities to make decisions and see what the results are with very simple choices, such as what to eat or what outfit to wear, the results are not of great consequence because there is another choice later and another opportunity to make a different selection. However, when you get into the Higher Dimensions, once you make a decision and bring forth a manifestation, making a correction can be a much more arduous process than it is at a lower level.

We wish for you to look each day at the decisions you have made and see how they have worked out for you. If you find that you have spoken words or had thoughts that were less than those that would benefit all concerned, you may wish to go back and think about how you could have reframed this situation to make it more harmonious for everyone. Then you can picture yourself uttering the words and doing the acts in harmony with your revised version of what you would like to have happen in the future. In this way you are programming your mind so that you are setting a pattern that will lead to harmonious processes at the higher levels.

Always remember that you are co-creating at whatever level on the path you happen to be. It may be at a beginning level, an intermediate level, or a very high level. Whatever step or level you are on, there is an opportunity to understand things from a much higher perspective. The more you focus on the subtle meanings of your thoughts and actions, the greater progress you will make, for you will understand what universal laws are at work and what subtle meanings accompany each thought and action you are taking.

There are many who act in the haste of the moment. This can be a mistake, for very often an untrained mind can make decisions that viewed in later light, would not be the best decision for that particular moment. However, when you train your mind to review your decisions each day, you are setting a course so that when you need to make a rapid decision, you are more likely to make a good or positive one that benefits all concerned. This leads to everyone benefitting from the Light surrounding the situation. The Light will be of a much higher quality and a much finer vibration. In this way, it can help to lift the consciousness of everyone affected by your decision and manifestation.

This is the way you can help others to progress along the path as you work in partnership with us. When they see that you are making decisions of a very high quality that benefit not only you but all concerned, they see that it is possible for everyone to come out with a winning solution that benefits all. This can lead to others deciding to try out this process with small decisions. Then when they have success, they can move to bigger decisions on higher levels.

This is what will change your planet and all of humanity. As more and more of you begin to operate in this manner, it will eventually reach critical mass, and everyone will instantly have the benefit of being surrounded with a higher consciousness. Whether they choose to partake of this higher consciousness still depends on their free will. However, you will be a great role model in showing them what is possible. Therefore, when they make their own individual decisions, you will know that you have done everything you can and will continue to do to help them along the path, just as we are helping you.

There are many who are ahead of you on the path who are helping you in the same way. They are coming to you with nudges and prompts all along the way. When you are thinking of a decision to be made, and you get an idea about a new way to do something, or a way that will be more beneficial to all, think of us because it is likely that one of us is coming to you to help you with a course of action.

There are many colors in the Rays of Light and the multidimensions. Depending on the decision to be made, you will likely receive a nudge from someone on that particular Ray or vibratory level who works with the type of decision to be made. You may be accustomed to working with only one or two of us, and we are always glad to come when you call. However, know that there may be others that we ask to come and assist in this process because just as you consult a specialist on your Earth Plane, we in the Higher Realms also have our own specialties. Therefore, we are able to offer you the greatest benefits of our advanced learning and knowledge so that you can move forward in the most beneficial way. We wish great success for you, and we are here to assist you in whatever way possible.

We are happy to be partners with you as you progress on your spiritual journey.

Know that you are greatly loved.

~ The Angelic Realm

Intention and Spiritual Growth

Very often, when we think about intention, we associate it with achieving some type of physical, concrete goal. Maybe we have a project we want to complete. We are very clear about what it will look like when it is completed and how we will feel. We have mastered that part of intention very nicely.

But what about setting an intention as part of spiritual advancement? We may have a vague idea about what we want to accomplish or what practices bring us joy. But we may have never consciously set an intention in the spiritual area.

Deciding what we want in the spiritual area can have many advantages. There are numerous opportunities calling to us – classes to take, webinars, packaged programs, conference calls, and so many more. If we are not careful, we can find ourselves filling our time with many of these activities. Then one day, we realize that even though each course or activity was good, it may not have led us to our desired goal. When we have a stated intention, we are able to discern which activities will help us achieve what we want. And, by not filling every moment going from one activity to another, we make space for our intentions to take us to our desired level of spiritual growth.

Another distinct advantage of setting an intention for spiritual advancement is that we are able to work more closely with the Higher Beings to move forward on our path. The Higher Beings want to work with us, but they need to know what we want. Do we want more peace in daily life? Do we want to learn a new healing technique for ourselves and others? Do we want to learn new wisdom teachings? How would we like to use this knowledge or skills? Or, do we want a deeper inner spiritual journey? Do we have a desire for fewer outward activities in order to have more time for inner work? Do we want to work at a multidimensional level?

When we set a clear intention for the next step on our spiritual path, the Higher Beings can bring opportunities to our attention. These may present themselves in the form of a book, a class, or someone who can assist us. They may also come to us in our quiet time or meditations.

In the past, I have sometimes skipped this step and later realized my mistake in not doing this important part. Now I have come to understand that setting a clear intention is an energetic principle that harnesses the vibratory forces around me. The extra time I spend on this step has helped me move forward and achieve the desired results on my path.

I experienced two personal examples of spiritual advancement as an intention as it related to pilgrimages to sacred sites.

On the first occasion, a pilgrimage to Peru was announced. Although I had always had Machu Picchu on my bucket list of sacred sites to visit, I was not called to sign up for it when the trip was first announced. I was puzzled at the lack of draw I felt, but I went with my gut feeling not to sign up immediately. Then, at the end of another pilgrimage to Banff, Canada, I felt an immediate call from the Star Beings to sign up for the trip to Peru. There was no mistaking the call. I felt it through my entire Being. They impressed on me that I would receive the advancement to a higher spiritual level on that pilgrimage and that they would be there to work with me.

So, I signed up. As I made extensive preparations for going to a higher altitude, I kept my focus on my spiritual intention to advance on my path and to work with the Star Beings.

They were true to their word. On the second day I was at Machu Picchu, they came through with a vision of healing work I had done there in a previous incarnation. My heart soared with the remembrance, and I knew that this would help to propel me to a higher level of spiritual work.

The second occurrence happened when I went to Tulum, Mexico. I knew Tulum contained sacred sites and that it was also close to the etheric retreats of the Archangels that I work with most closely, Archangel Zadkiel and Lady Amethyst. My intention on that trip, which was a writing retreat, was to propel my writing to the next spiritual level. After several days of the retreat, the Star Beings came through and brought me many beautiful writings on a multidimensional level. These writings included messages to be shared with others along with personal guidance. I was elated!

I had received more than I could have imagined!

As I reviewed what had occurred on both occasions, I realized that I had set my spiritual intention and had asked for the appropriate Beings of Light to assist me. I had remained open to receive and had expressed gratitude for what they shared.

When we set clear spiritual intentions, the benefits ripple throughout our entire Being. We increase our spiritual growth, and we can more easily access multidimensional levels. The opportunities to reach higher and higher levels are limitless when we continue to focus on spiritual growth.

◆ ◆ ◆

Clarity on Your Spiritual Path

~ Inspiration from The Angelic Realm ~

Beloved Ones,

You are living in times of great opportunity for spiritual advancement. Many of the old rules of having to wait a certain length of time at each step have been set aside in order for those with great desire to make rapid advancement on the path of ascension. The way has been cleared for you by those who have gone ahead and set an energetic course for you. It is now up to each individual to select the path of greatest fit and to follow it with a great passion for advancement and ascension.

The intensity of your desire will help to determine

how rapidly you are able to move forward. Your desires are your intentions. From an energetic perspective your intentions are energy that radiates out from you. This energy draws like energy back to you. It puts you on a wave or channel of similar energy that matches your vibration or frequency that you have sent forth based on your desires. The stronger your intentions or desires, the stronger the energy that you will draw back to you. This is why it is vitally important for you to be clear in your desires so that you will draw back what you would like.

It is important that you monitor your thoughts and emotions, for what you think and feel is what you send out. An idle thought on its own may not seem very important to you at the time, but no matter how idle or small it is, it sends out its own energetic charge. The unit of energy that it sends out will draw back a similar unit of like energy to you. This effect is especially magnified at a multidimensional level.

If you send out mixed messages of what you want to the Universe, mixed energy is what will be returned to you. If one moment you have an intense desire to move forward on your path and the next moment you don't want to spend the necessary time on your spiritual practice, this sends a mixed message, and mixed energy is what you will receive. The path has been muddled because the energy you sent forth was mixed. Obstacles may appear in your path. These represent the mixed energy from your mixed desires.

However, if you are clear about your path, all of the energy that you send forth will be of a like vibration. It will draw back to you energy of a similar vibration. For example, if you have an intense desire to move forward on your spiritual path and you exhibit a willingness to set aside a time for your spiritual practice and then follow through on this, you are sending a clear message to the Universe that you are serious about moving forward. Your energy is clear, and you are sending a unified message because your intentions and actions are congruent. You are definite about what you want, and you are following through on your intentions and reinforcing them with your actions. This sends a clear, unified message, and you receive clear, similar energy back.

In practical terms you may gain additional insights about your path, you may see a book that will further enlighten you, or you may meet someone from whom you will receive nuggets of wisdom.

You may even have new Higher Beings who present themselves to assist you. When you are clear about your path, you are opening yourself up to receive assistance from the Higher Realms.

Being clear about your path does not mean accepting everything that comes to you on blind faith. As always, it is important to validate everything that you receive in your heart center to see if it resonates with you. If it feels right, you may decide to use what you have received. If it does not feel right or you are not sure, you may set it aside. If it is right for you, it will present itself again later. If it is not right for you, then you have not acted on something that truly was not what was best for you. It is important to be true to what resonates with you as you are moving forward. As you practice seeing and feeling what resonates with you, the recognition of these signals will become easier. You will be tuning in to your inner promptings about your path. Your clarity about your path will become sharper and more refined.

When you are clear about your path, this acts as a barometer against which you can measure whatever comes to you or what action you wish to take. If someone suggests a certain activity to you and you are clear about your chosen path, this will be your measuring stick by which to judge whether the activity is right for you and whether it is a good fit for your path. Just because the activity is right for someone else does not automatically mean that it is right for you. The activity in and of itself may be fine. The crucial part is whether it will help you advance on your chosen path. Each person's path is unique, and the activities that will fit each person's path will vary. Being clear about your own path will be your barometer and measuring stick for making decisions about activities.

This also applies to new spiritual guides who come to you. Is their energy a good fit for you? Is it positive and uplifting? Discernment still applies at the multidimensional level.

Because the energy manifests more rapidly at higher levels, discernment takes on an even more critical role.

The more you practice tuning in to what is right for you, the clearer your barometer will be. If you are not sure how to read your barometer and what its signals are, you can think back to things with which you completely resonate. Notice how your body feels.

What type of feeling do you have in your solar plexus, in your heart area, or all over your body? Do you feel tense and anxious or relaxed and happy? By tuning in to things that already are right for you, you can learn exactly how you receive the signals for new things that may come your way. Then when something new presents itself, you will know whether you are receiving a clear signal that the new situation may be something to explore further or whether to let it go and not act on it. If you do not receive a clear signal, you may set it aside and ask for further clarification. When you make the request for further clarification, remain alert for the answer to come. It may come from something that someone else says, from a book, from a billboard, or from some other unexpected source. When you remain open to receive after you have asked for the clarification, you are allowing further signals to come your way.

If you initially begin a course of action and then decide that it does not resonate with you, that is your signal to modify it. Many times you may begin an activity, and it may feel right for a time. Then it no longer resonates with you. This is your indication that a correction in course is necessary. The activities that support your spiritual path may change as you evolve.

If you can decide what specifically doesn't feel right to you about the activity, this learning can be applied to future situations. Look at everything as a lesson that will help you further clarify your path. In this way you can strengthen what does feel right, and you can eliminate what doesn't feel right. This develops your ability of discernment to know what is right for you. This ability will become increasingly important as you progress on your ascension path, especially at a multidimensional level. You will be able to discern the appropriateness of an activity for you much more quickly. You will know what your individual signals of resonance are and can act on them with confidence. This is a skill that is developed like any other skill. The more you develop this skill, the greater your confidence in it will become.

As you develop clarity in your discernment about what is right for you, you may find that you are also developing a greater sense of inner peace and calmness. You are becoming a much more inner-directed Being because you have developed the ability to recognize what is right for you.

A periodic review of your path may also help you

clarify where you are. If you have developed your barometer of knowing whether something feels right for you, this can greatly assist you in your review. As you look at where you are on your path, think about whether you are still excited about your direction. If you are still excited, what are the things that are keeping you feeling that way? Are there things that you no longer feel excited about? Are they things you can modify or change, or are they things that can be eliminated? Everyone has certain parts of their path that may be necessary but may not be as exciting as others. The key is to look at those things as contributing to the success of your overall path. By framing them in a new light, they may begin to appear as contributing to your success rather than as a hindrance. Of course, if you find an activity that is not necessary and no longer excites you, then you have the option to make a change. Everything needs to be evaluated from the perspective of your highest good and the greatest good of all. This keeps your actions aligned with Divine Will and allows us to assist you for the greatest good of all.

The energy is moving very rapidly, and the more you can develop and practice clarity on your path, the more you can use this wondrous new energy to propel you forward as you ascend. It is a time of marvelous opportunity.

Beloveds, we are happy to see you progressing on your spiritual path, and we are here to assist you with your goals.

Know that you are greatly loved.

~ The Angelic Realm

Staying Focused

—✕✕✕—

As a seasoned traveler on the path, you may have experienced times where you set a clear intention for your next step, and everything went well for a time. You were excited about your path and the next step, and you eagerly worked on it each day. You could see and even feel your dreams in a manifested form.

Then you encountered some rough patches. Maybe something didn't work out as you had expected or hoped it would. That particular part of your path may have required more time and effort than you thought it would, and you became discouraged.

Distractions may have appeared and temporarily eased your mind about your intended course of action. Perhaps another course of study attracted you. Someone may have suggested an activity that sounded appealing.

Or you may have asked yourself whether the amount of effort required for the next step was worth all of your energy, even though it was really what your heart desired. You may have even felt like putting your dreams on the shelf.

At these crucial points, maintaining focus can help you stay on your desired path and move through those challenging moments. Sometimes the darkest moments appear just before the dawn.

As you are aware as a seasoned traveler, one of the easiest ways to remain focused is to monitor your thoughts and place your attention on your desired intention and outcome.

The more you practice this, the easier it will be to move forward on your desired path. You will be less easily distracted, and you will make progress on your intentions.

Doing this may seem a bit mechanical and automated at first, but soon it will be your default pattern, and it may even feel natural. You will be in the flow.

Your thoughts play a large role in being true to yourself. They set the stage for everything that comes later.

A thought leads to an emotion which leads to an

action. As you know, sometimes this happens with lightning speed. At the multidimensional levels, our thoughts manifest more quickly because the energy is vibrating at a higher frequency.

If we encounter something that triggers an old pattern in us, we can go from trigger to thought to emotion to action in the blink of an eye. Then we stop ourselves and wonder how this happened and how we allowed ourselves to be drawn off course.

When we process this and work backward from the action to the emotion to the thought to the trigger, we can see what happened. When we maintain clearly focused thoughts, we are less likely to be drawn off course.

Taking time to re-focus on what called you to the next step on your path can be a place to begin. Go into a meditative state, and recall in detail how this path makes your heart sing. Maybe it gives you more time for yourself, an opportunity to deepen your spiritual practice, or a way to put your skills to use for the greater good of humanity.

Sometimes, when you focus on the longings of your path at a heart level, the obstacles seem to disappear, and once again, you are ready to take the next step on your path.

I have experienced the importance of staying focused as I have prepared for spiritual pilgrimages.

Traveling on pilgrimages has been one part of my spiritual path. I love visiting sacred sites and tuning in to see what I will receive.

I have been fortunate to visit many such spots in Bolivia, England, Scotland, Egypt, Ireland, Greece, Israel, Jordan, Canada, Peru, Mexico, and the United States. On these pilgrimages I have had connections with the Higher Realms and recognition of various past life experiences that have contributed to my Soul growth.

As much as I love pilgrimages, preparing for them can often feel tedious to me. Decisions around clothes, shoes, first aid supplies, airline flights, and many other smaller details often lead me to feel overwhelmed and to question just why I made the decision to take the upcoming journey. At those times I place additional focus on my intention for the pilgrimage, and I regain my momentum for dealing with the details.

I am reminded that small obstacles really do disappear when we remain focused on our intention for the next step of our path.

The more we focus on the reason we selected an intention and how we feel when we picture it as completed, the more easily we can stay focused.

❖ ❖ ❖

Focus Your Thoughts

~ Inspiration from The Angelic Realm ~

Beloved Ones,

In the current times of higher vibrational energy, it is important to focus your thoughts. Much new energy is reaching your planet, and this brings the opportunity for you to manifest your desires much more quickly. It also offers you the opportunity to ascend to higher levels of consciousness.

Focusing your thoughts can be compared to selecting a television station. If you tune your thoughts to a frequency of daily mundane situations, then this is what will fill your consciousness. This is the vibration that you will send out, and this is what you will attract to you. The stronger your focus on these types of situations, the more of these situations you will attract to you. It is the Universal Law of Attraction that like attracts like.

However, if you select a frequency that is motivating and inspiring and you tune your thoughts to this, your consciousness will be filled by that particular frequency. Your attention and consciousness will be focused on thoughts of motivation and inspiration.

If you wish to have more peace and harmony in your life, you can begin by thinking about peace and harmony. Picture peaceful situations in your life, and then feel the peaceful vibrations of those situations. The more you visualize these situations and feel their vibrations, the more they will manifest in your daily life because your thoughts and feelings are creating your reality.

The vibrations of your thoughts also radiate out into the multidimensions.

If you wish to be in closer communication with us in the Realms of Light, think about us and feel our loving presence. We are delighted when you want to communicate with us. The veils between the realms are thinning, and communication is much easier. It is simply a matter of adjusting your frequency to be closer to ours. As you raise your frequency, we can adjust ours slightly so that communication is possible.

Keeping your frequency at a higher level during your day-to-day routine will make communication with us much easier because a high vibration or frequency will be your default pattern. You will be able to tune in to us more easily. You may even feel us around you as you go throughout your day.

To set your frequency at a higher level, begin with the intention for this to occur. When you want to establish a new pattern, a clearly stated intention is the first step. Then begin to visualize what your intended goal would look like. Picture it in your mind. Make it the picture of highest good for all because this will carry a higher vibration.

Then focus on what your intended outcome would feel like. A high vibrational outcome might include love, joy, peace, and happiness as well as highest good.

Once you have set your intended outcome, focus your thoughts and feelings on it. Random thoughts will bring random results. Focused thoughts are much stronger and are more likely to bring the desired results. Highly focused thoughts can have a laser-like effect in manifesting your desired goal or outcome.

If you begin to find your thoughts wandering into a random pattern, simply redirect them back to your desired outcome. The more you practice this, the easier it will be to keep your thoughts focused on what you want.

The higher the frequency of your desired outcome, the higher the frequency of your thoughts needs to be. If you are wishing for peace and harmony in a situation, release thoughts of judgment or anger around anyone or anything in the situation. Focus on seeing the highest and the best in everyone and everything to keep your thoughts at a high frequency.

When you focus your thoughts and feelings on situations and things of a higher vibrational frequency, this is what you will attract to you. Set your intention for highest good as you focus on your desires.

Beloveds, we are here to assist you in staying focused on your intentions and your path. Call on us to help you as you move forward.

Know that you are greatly loved.

~ The Angelic Realm

Expressing Gratitude

———◇◇◇———

As a seasoned traveler on the spiritual path, you are well acquainted with the practice of expressing gratitude. We have been taught from an early age to thank someone when they have done something nice for us. It is one of the social graces that helps a society to function and a community to support each other.

In addition to gratitude having a social grace aspect, there is also a higher spiritual principle at work.

Expressing gratitude begins with a thought of appreciation for what you have received. Your gift may be large such as someone providing assistance to you, or it may be something small such as a compliment. No matter the size of the gift you receive, acknowledging it and expressing gratitude completes a circle of energy. The giver has contributed a portion of their energy to you, and you are expressing appreciation for what they have given and you have received. If gratitude is not expressed, the energetic circle has not been completed. It is left open and unfinished.

When the circle is left open energetically, there is a void and the energy of what was given may dissipate.

However, when gratitude is expressed, the circle is complete. The energy that was given initially has reached its intended point, and it has been acknowledged by the receiver. This frees up additional energy to begin again in a giving and receiving sequence.

The feeling that accompanies the expression of gratitude places both the giver and the receiver in a higher vibrational state. Gratitude carries a high spiritual energy, and it opens the door for advancement.

It could be compared to a spiral of energy. The giving begins at one point and circles around to the receiver. When the receiver expresses gratitude, the circle is complete. The next circle of evolution and manifestation begins at a higher vibratory level because both the giver and the receiver have experienced a spiritual uplifting. As this process continues, the energy rises to higher and higher levels.

Expressing gratitude is important not only on the

third-dimensional level but also at each level of the multidimensions.

When we ask the Higher Beings of Light to work with us and assist us, an exchange of energy takes place. We send forth our request, and they respond by assisting us in whatever way is appropriate and is for highest good.

Our request to them may be for something large such as helping to manifest a goal, or it may be a small one such as helping us find a good parking place. No matter what their assistance has been, it is important to acknowledge it and express gratitude. Then a working relationship occurs. It is similar to a neighbor helping another neighbor. This is just a difference of degree because it is a Higher Being assisting us on the Earth Plane. It has occurred multidimensionally.

The more we express gratitude, the stronger the working relationship will be. It will develop into a true co-creative partnership.

On a spiritual level, expressing gratitude allows the free flow of energy to continue. If gratitude is not expressed, it could be compared to energy flowing through a copper wire and suddenly reaching a blockage that stops the energy.

When we express gratitude, we feel good. We have acknowledged what the other person or Being has done for us. Our exchange of energy is the love and appreciation we send back to them. The circle is then complete, and the energy is ready for its next evolution.

◆ ◆ ◆

Gratitude

~ Inspiration from The Angelic Realm ~

Beloved Ones,

You are living in times where it is very important to be conscious of all that you are sending forth. The aspect of gratitude is one area where intentional expression can greatly assist your ascension process.

Gratitude for what you have received is very important from an energetic standpoint. Your thoughts and words carry a vibration, or a frequency, and an energetic flow. When you express gratitude in thoughts or words, this sends forth an energetic flow. In the process of sending forth gratitude, you are setting up a chain of energy to lift you to a higher vibration and to a level to which you aspire on your ascension path.

When you ask us to assist you in the accomplishment of a goal or to bring something forth to you or someone else, we are most happy to assist in this when it is for your greatest good and the highest good of all. We may offer our assistance by giving you prompts or nudges to take a certain action, or we may give you an idea that can be manifested to help everyone concerned on a larger scale. We are always viewing your requests from a higher perspective.

As you move higher and higher in your vibratory level, your requests also rise to a higher harmonic. They become more inclusive of what will benefit the many rather than the few. This shows that you have progressed by first filling yourself with Love and Light and then asking for blessings for others.

As we assist you in manifesting your requests, this gives us great pleasure, for we wish to see you prosper and be happy. Many of you are very good at asking for what you desire. This is a proper step, for you need to be clear about what you would like so that we can be of the greatest assistance.

As children you were taught to express thanks for

what you had received. Expressing gratitude goes beyond the polite manners that you were taught growing up. There is a far higher energetic component to the act of expressing gratitude. First, when you express gratitude for your blessings, you acknowledge that your requests have been heard. You are letting us know that you are aware that we have heard your requests and have responded.

Sometimes, we may send forth an expression of help that is somewhat different than what you had requested. It may produce the same end result, but the method of the assistance is different. When you express gratitude for the assistance that we have given, this lets us know that you are aware that we were working with you to accomplish your desires. Asking and receiving and then expressing gratitude is a two-way process. You ask, we assist, and you express gratitude for what has been given. This keeps a constant flow of energy moving for you to ask, for us to assist, and for you to receive. The component of gratitude is what keeps the process flowing.

Compare this to a moving stream of water. The stream of water is the flow of blessings. Your desires are the channel that moves the water in a certain direction. When you express gratitude for what has been given, this helps to move the water in the desired direction. It adds energy to assist the stream and sets a clear channel through which the water can flow.

When you forget to express gratitude, this can be compared to a dam that stops the flow of the stream. At first the water begins to accumulate in a small pond. This is deceptive because you may think that because you have an accumulating quantity of water, nothing else is required. However, after a time the water begins to stagnate because there is no flow. Any fresh water that comes in is mixed with the stagnant water, and the entire pond becomes murky. The water that has accumulated does not move forward to reach its intended destination or goal. Others who are expecting the stream to reach them are looking in desperation for the water. Those who originally helped in the flow of the water do not know whether their efforts were helpful. Therefore, they may be reluctant to offer further assistance because they do not know whether they did the right thing.

The same can be said for us in the Higher Realms. We are most happy to offer our assistance, especially when it is used for your highest good and the greatest good of all. Your expression of gratitude to us is what keeps the assistance flowing. When you express gratitude, you are acknowledging that this is a partnership between you and those of us in the Higher Realms. You are also letting us know that the assistance we provided was helpful for you to reach the desired outcome of your request.

When you express gratitude, this energetically raises your vibration. You usually feel happy as a result of what has taken place. A joyful feeling raises your vibration. It allows you to see a higher perspective and to tap into even greater possibilities. It lifts your vision to a level that can help Mother Earth and all of humanity. When you express gratitude, you are also feeling a sense of Love. The Love vibration is the greatest one that exists. It can remove obstacles and provide hope to many. This lifts your vibration even higher. The more that you express sincere gratitude, the higher your vibration will be lifted. A sense of sincere gratitude places you in a state to receive even more.

Each day think of the many things for which you are grateful – a roof over your head, food to eat, transportation, family and friends, and the ability to know that you are connected to an energetic flow from the Supreme Creator down to yourself. This awareness will allow your consciousness to rise to higher and higher levels. You may express your gratitude in words or feelings or both. The quality of the feeling, whether with or without words, is what will allow you to ascend most easily.

We in the Higher Realms are aware of your Energetic Signature, and this is the method by which we receive your requests. If your words do not match your vibrations and energy level, we are confused by what you really want. Therefore, when you express gratitude with a sincere and heartfelt feeling of Love and appreciation, we know that we have been working together with you as a team to accomplish your desires.

The more you express gratitude, the more we can be of assistance. It is a partnership between you and those of us in the Higher Realms. Seeing you move forward on your path of ascension brings happiness to us, for we know that we are all working together to raise the consciousness of humanity and for the betterment of Mother Earth and the Universe.

Your powerful and loving gratitude is beautiful as it ripples throughout the multidimensions for the greatest good of all.

Beloved Ones, we eagerly anticipate your requests and your expressions of gratitude so that we may continue our harmonious work together with you.

Know that you are greatly loved.

~ The Angelic Realm

PART 3

REFINING YOUR PATH

You Are Constantly Evolving

—✕✕✕—

You have been enjoying your redesigned path, and you have felt that you are being true to yourself.

Then one day, you sense something different. Something feels off. It is a similar feeling that you experienced before you created your current path. At first, it may be a passing thought or feeling. Then the sensation grows louder. Finally, you decide to examine it more closely.

Suddenly, you are asking yourself, "Why do my goals feel stale? Why do they no longer excite me? Why doesn't my path call to me anymore? Why do I feel a sense of boredom or dread when I think about it? What happened to my happiness?"

If you find yourself asking these questions, this may be a signal that you need to examine your path and see whether you want to make another adjustment.

You are constantly evolving. It is an ongoing process. You are not the same person today that you were yesterday. You have completed that level of learning and understanding, and now you are ready for a new exploration. Every moment brings new insights.

At this point on your path, you are a seasoned traveler in your spiritual work. You have explored many concepts and modalities. You have retained those that you are drawn to and have discarded those that no longer feel like you. You have a clear idea of what resonates with you.

But now, you may be asking, "What next? Have I accomplished or done everything I came here to do? Do I really want to forge ahead, or do I want to take it easy and let others do the heavy spiritual work?" You may feel bored with what you decided to do, even very recently. You may even wonder if you pause on your path whether you will lose your spiritual direction.

If you find yourself asking these questions or having these feelings, it may mean that you have completed your current level of learning and mastery, and now you are moving to a higher level. Your Soul is presenting you with new opportunities.

It is normal to question yourself at these points on your ascension path.

This provides an ideal time to determine what you really want for the next step on your spiritual journey.

You have an internal compass and center of guidance that you have likely refined to a highly functioning point. Now it is time to give yourself permission to use it.

You no longer have to stay on the same path you were on last year, last week, or even yesterday.

I, like you, have experienced my own process of evolving. My path has taken many twists and turns. At each point along the way, I was exactly where I needed to be for the particular lessons and service for the evolution of my Soul.

Sometimes I remained longer at one point than was necessary. I would feel a gentle nudge from the Universe that it was time for me to take the next step. This would come in the form of wondering if I really wanted to commit my time to the extra effort required on that step, or I found myself just wanting to do nothing and take a time out. I would question whether I was on the right path.

When I paid attention to those gentle nudges and made adjustments, things progressed smoothly. However, if I lingered too long, stronger prompts would occur. Sometimes, this manifested as a brief illness or a feeling of unease before participating in an activity.

Fortunately, I eventually got the message that I had learned what I needed to at that point on my path and had made whatever contributions to the greater good that I was supposed to make. It was okay for me to take the next step.

This was sometimes daunting. It isn't always easy to leave a familiar activity to experience a new one.

Doing things that are familiar can be comforting. I knew what to expect, and I knew I had the knowledge and skills to perform them well. How could I leave that to begin something new? Did I have what it takes to make that change? What if others didn't approve of my change or adjustment?

I have been very fortunate along the way to have supportive friends and family who encourage me. And, of course, I have my guides and teachers in the Higher Realms.

Each time I embarked on the next step of my path

or made an adjustment, I felt exhilarated. My energy felt clear, and I was ready to make the adjustment.

One adjustment I made was to reapportion the way I allocated my time for teaching and writing. I had previously made teaching workshops the central feature of my work. I love interacting with participants as we explore new concepts and tools and discuss how they have helped us.

However, a gentle nudge was growing within me that was encouraging me to allocate more time to writing. I would wake up with a knowing that the Higher Beings wanted to communicate with me and that they were encouraging me to write more.

But how would I do this and continue with teaching? Did I have to choose one and abandon the other? No, I simply needed to adjust the amount of time I was giving to each activity.

I decided to allocate more time to writing and reduce my teaching schedule for a brief period of time. Then I could make another adjustment and begin teaching what I was receiving in my writing. It would be an ongoing process of balancing and adjusting. After all, I was free to set my own schedule and do what the Universe was prompting me to do to be of greatest service at that time.

I felt a great relief after I made this decision. It felt fluid. Nothing was set in concrete, and most important, I was being true to myself. I was adjusting my path as I changed and as my work changed. I was being true to the most current version of myself.

When we give ourselves permission to change, we are honoring ourselves and the beautiful, multidimensional Beings of Light that we are.

❖ ❖ ❖

Remaining True to Your Own Path

~ Inspiration from The Angelic Realm ~

Beloved Ones,

This is indeed an auspicious time for all of humanity. All of you are being given the opportunity as to whether to move forward. In choosing how to move forward, you are being allowed to move as rapidly or as slowly as you would like, for this is the time of the individual decision.

It is no longer a requirement that each person follow the same path. This is causing much consternation among many of you because in the past the herd mentality has been the rule. In this day and time that is no longer the case. Individuals must select their own path and remain true to themselves as they walk forward on that path. This can lead to great feelings of separation and loneliness if the path chosen is at odds with what you have been walking or with what others have been expecting you to walk.

However, each person will be on their own path. Therefore, it is very important for you to honor who you are. You have a Divine mission of your own, and to fulfill this mission, it is important for you to do what you feel called to do. It may be that your path will take you on a similar path to that on which you have been, or you may move in a completely different direction. The important thing is to honor what is in your heart and in your Soul as you move forward. Realize that you must remain strong and calm in your center, for there will be some who may try to dissuade you from your path. They will try to tell you that you are wrong and that you should be moving in a different direction.

Beloveds, remember that you were never all supposed to move in the same direction at the same time. This was necessary as humanity came out of the dark ages, but now you are in enlightened times. Therefore, it is time for each individual to answer what resonates with them and to move forward in that direction. When you maintain a calm center, you are able to move forward in your own direction with satisfaction. You will know that you are going in the correct direction for you because you will feel happiness and joy in your heart. You will also feel that you are doing what is right for you, and at the same time, you will feel that you are performing a service for humanity. If everyone followed the same path, there would be some things that would remain undone because there are many paths. This is a greater assurance that all of the tasks and paths will be fulfilled.

The important thing is to remember to fulfill your own path to the greatest of your ability and to do it with a happy heart. It does not matter whether it is what society considers a lowly position or a high one. The important thing is that you perform your path to the greatest of your ability and with Love and compassion for all with whom you come in contact. This is the key that will help each person to move forward on their path. The Love and compassion that come forth from your heart will assure that you are moving forward in higher and higher directions. As you do this, you will find new opportunities opening to you. You will know which one is right for you by the way you feel when you encounter it.

Yes, Beloved Ones, it does take courage to follow your own path, for this is indeed a time of stepping out and stepping into your true identity and claiming your birthright of who you are. You are indeed magnificent Souls, and we rejoice in the fact that you have chosen to move forward on your own path, for this shows that we are all coming closer and closer together. We may come to you during your sleep time, or you may hear our whispers or feel our nudges during your meditation times. The important thing is to be true to yourself and to move forward on the path that you feel is the correct one for you. Also, remember to exhibit Love and compassion for those who have chosen other paths. You may do this by having Love and compassion for yourself first, for when you do this, you become more secure in your own path. Then you can be more secure when others select paths different from your own.

Beloveds, you are moving higher and higher in the Realms of Light, and you are indeed a shining star on your path. You are a great inspiration to others.

We are here to work with you whenever you call on us.

Know that you are greatly loved.

~ The Angelic Realm

Letting Go

$—\infty\infty—$

When you decide to make an adjustment in your path, you begin the process of letting go. Sometimes this is easy, and other times it can be hard. Whatever your experience may be, it is a process of sorting out what is right for you at this time on your path.

You can use the same process that you did when you made your last major adjustment. By now, you are familiar with the steps to take. Your biggest decision is what to keep and what to let go.

Making an adjustment at this point brings the challenges it did earlier. How do you explain to others your refined path? What are their expectations, and what will they think? Is this a factor for you, or are you comfortable letting the chips fall where they may? Will this affect your income or your circle of friends?

These are all factors in your adjustment, and only you can decide what is right for you. As you ponder these conditions, you may want to think about nonattachment as it relates to your decisions.

When you are not attached to external factors, your decisions will be easier. You will be inner directed. However, if others are directly affected by your choices, you may have more of a dilemma.

For example, if you are teaching classes and this is a major source of your income, and you decide to scale back your schedule, how will this affect your ability to pay your bills? Are there others who are depending on you to keep your current schedule, or are you only responsible for yourself?

If you are coaching and decide to scale back your schedule, how will this affect your clients? Is there a way you can do this to meet both your needs and theirs?

As I made the decision to temporarily readjust the balance of my time between writing and teaching, I had to let go of being concerned about what others would think. Fortunately, I have had very positive responses to my decision, and I have felt supported.

There are many decisions as you go forward. Only you can decide what to keep, what to let go, and what to adjust. When you stay in tune with the wisdom of your heart and your inner guidance, you will have an inner knowing that you are making the adjustments that are right for you and are for highest good.

◆ ◆ ◆

Letting Go and Allowing

~ Inspiration from The Angelic Realm ~

Beloved Ones,

There are many energetic changes occurring on your planet. Each time there is an energy shift, existing energetic patterns are affected. These shifts may enhance an existing pattern, or they may cause great disruption. You may experience this shift as peaceful if the change enhances the pattern, or you may feel distress if the change is not harmonious for you. You may find that the patterns are constantly changing and that before you can adjust to the current change, another one has occurred.

Your physical, emotional, mental, and spiritual bodies, or layers of energy, are constantly working to accommodate the changes. The new incoming energy has a much different pattern and frequency, and this allows you to continue on your ascension path.

These shifts can affect your priorities, intentions, thoughts, and actions. They may extend to relationships and long-established patterns and ways of doing things.

The new, higher frequency energy tends to shake things up and invites you to a new way of being. It is offering you an opportunity to take a fresh look at areas where you may have been considering an adjustment.

The new energy is inviting you to move to a higher level of consciousness.

It is inviting you to consider letting go of what no longer serves you and allowing yourself to flow with new possibilities.

When these energy shifts are taking place, it is important to be aware of how you feel personally with each shift. A regular assessment of where you are on your path allows you to decide whether you wish to make any changes in your current patterns and practices.

A shift in letting go and allowing may be very simple, or it may be more profound.

For example, it may be a gentle decision to change

your time of getting up in the morning or taking a different route when you are going to a familiar location.

It may be feeling drawn to read something that presents a new way of thinking about topics.

Or, it may be more profound, such as a move to a new location.

Whenever you are assessing any area of your life on your current path, the key is to be open and allow yourself to imagine other possibilities. This does not mean you must select each option you imagine. It is rather tuning in with your heart and mind simultaneously to determine what the right fit is for you at any given moment.

When you do this, you are letting go of rigid thinking and allowing yourself to flow with the new energy.

Then you are able to determine whether you wish to make changes in any area of your path. You may find that you are exactly where you want to be. If you find that you wish to make a change in any area, you are able to flow with the change in a more gentle manner.

When you allow yourself to flow with the new energy, you are remaining open to new thoughts and ideas. You begin to see new ways of being, which can lead to moving higher in consciousness.

The key to the process is to be open and allow. When you do this in a relaxed state of being, you are more likely to receive flashes of insight and messages from your guides.

Then you can evaluate whether these insights and messages feel right for you and are logical for you. Your process of discernment increases during this evaluation. You become more aware of what is right for you and what is not. If you receive flashes of insight or messages that you do not feel are right for you, you can simply discard them or set them aside for later consideration.

As you let go and allow, you are in a state of flow with the energy. Your consciousness increases and rises, and your awareness expands to a multidimensional level.

When you ask for the highest and best for all as you do this process, your Light shines throughout the dimensions.

Beloveds, we are happy that you are open to letting

go and allowing as the new energy enters your environment. We are sending you Light as you continue on your ascension path.

Know that you are greatly loved.

~ The Angelic Realm

The Power of Being Present

—✕—

As you are refining your path, you have an added bonus when you are fully present. This is a powerful technique because you are tuned in to what is going on at the present moment.

You are not concerned about what happened last year, last week, yesterday, or what will happen tomorrow. You are a different person than you were at those previous points, and you may be at a new point in the future.

The present moment allows you to be who you are now and to adjust your path so that it meets your current needs. Often, we have to take a step in the present moment before we can get to our next step. If we focus on where we were in the past, this can hinder our progress.

In the present moment, all possibilities can be examined.

When you remain in the present moment, you are fully aware of where you are, what you want, and what feels right for you. You can more easily receive the subtle prompts from the Universe.

For example, if you are browsing in a bookstore and you are thinking about what to have for dinner, you may completely miss seeing a book that could prompt you for the next step on your path.

When you are talking with someone, if you are focused on what you will say next rather than fully listening to what they are saying, you may miss a crucial point of information that could be a message from your guides.

In each case, the messages and prompts are subtle. The further you progress on your path, the more subtle the messages will be. When you remain in the present moment, you are able to receive them as they occur. You do not have to wait until later when they may be stronger and more pronounced. You can receive them immediately and evaluate them for their relevance to your changes.

I like to use this process on a regular basis. I sit in meditation and ask my guides and the Universe what I need to know at the present time. Then I wait quietly with my eyes closed. Usually, they respond quickly, so I like to keep a pen and paper beside me.

Sometimes their responses are to continue certain practices that I have been doing or to add more time to a certain practice. For example, they may encourage me to add more meditation times during the day. At other times, they may encourage me to read a new book, or they may help me to view my current path from a higher level. I can more easily receive their information when I am fully present.

Then I am able to see if their suggestions feel right for me at the present time. If they do, I know that I need to take action rather than setting their guidance aside. I am reminded that the suggestions that are given are for conditions currently in my life and not what has occurred in the past.

When we set an intention to be fully present, our consciousness can direct us in this way. The more we are fully present, the more we are able to receive guidance for highest good.

❖ ❖ ❖

Being Fully Present

~ Inspiration from The Angelic Realm ~

Beloved Ones,

The incoming energy is moving rapidly to a higher frequency. It is calling you to absorb it and integrate it into your Being. It is calling you to a higher consciousness.

As this new energy enters your field, you are being given the opportunity to learn new insights for your progression. They are very subtle and require your full attention to gain the complete benefits from them.

As a multidimensional Being of Light, your energy field is fluid. It is not a fixed point of time but rather a constantly changing and evolving field. It is designed for progression and harkens back to the time when you were subtle energy and had not yet become solid matter.

As such, the more you remain open to new insights, the more rapidly you progress on your ascension path.

One way to do this is to be fully present.

Being fully present means to focus on the task at hand. It is not thinking about what you did yesterday or what will take place tomorrow. It is focusing on the present moment.

This does not mean that you are oblivious to what is taking place. It means that you have expanded your awareness to encompass the past, the present, and the future simultaneously. You have gained the ability to expand and contract your awareness as needed. You are aware that linear time is a third dimensional concept, and this frees you to focus on the present moment. You are a point of Light in the great cosmos, and events are points of energy in this process.

This realization allows you to focus on the point of energy that is currently taking place.

When you are fully present in the moment, you are able to receive the subtle insights from the Universe. These prompts may come in the form of a thought that passes through like a gentle breeze. When they enter your awareness, they may seem to be a curiosity or a questioning of where that came from or what it means.

When you are focused on the present moment, these

insights remain in your consciousness and are there to guide you at the time you need them.

It is as if your energy field is always open to receive these insights, and it adapts to reflect on them and accommodate them as appropriate. This allows you to move forward because you are open to receive the incoming energy.

To remain open, it is important to be willing to receive the new insights. If you are attached to a preconceived idea of how things are supposed to be, it will be more difficult to recognize the insights as they occur. However, when you are not attached to a certain concept, you can flow with the new awareness as it occurs. This allows you to progress with ease and grace. The new awareness enters your energy field, and because it is fluid and flowing, it is assimilated as appropriate.

This does not mean that you automatically accept every new insight. It does mean that you are aware of it. If you are unsure of what it means for you, you can place it in a holding pattern for further reflection.

In addition to being open to receiving new insights, you can enhance this process by focusing on what is taking place in the present moment. Be fully focused on what you are doing. It does not mean multitasking to the extent that you have no concept of what is occurring around you. It means that you are focused on the task at hand, and this allows you to receive incoming insights.

If you find your attention straying from what is going on, you can simply pause, take a few deep breaths in and out, and return your focus to the present moment.

The more you practice this, the more automatic it will become. You will relax into being fully present, and you will be at one with All That Is.

Know that you are greatly loved.

~ The Angelic Realm

The Call to Nurture Yourself

As a seasoned spiritual traveler, you have accomplished much as you are moving forward on your path. You have communicated with the Beings of Light in the Higher Realms, and you have worked in a co-creative role with them.

This process may have occurred either consciously or unconsciously.

At some point, you may be asking yourself if you are nurturing yourself or if you are putting all of your focus on others.

You may even wonder if this is all there is, especially now that you are refining your path.

When thoughts such as these occur, you may want to consider taking time to nurture yourself and regain the balance between self and others.

When you are excited about the work you are doing, it is natural to want to put all of your energy into it. The focus and excitement can build to a point where you forget to nurture yourself in the process.

Then suddenly one day, you may realize that you are exhausted, and you may be questioning if this is really what you want to do. You may feel that it's all too much.

This is a sure signal to take time to nurture yourself and regain the balance between self and work, between your inner world and the outer world, and between self and others.

Sometimes when this occurs, we may wonder if it is being selfish to take this time for ourselves. It's the same thought that reared its head when we decided to modify our path. After all, we may have others who are depending on us. Again, do we want to risk their disappointment and disapproval, or do we want to take care of ourselves? The answer to this is very individual and depends on your own circumstances.

One way to look at this is that we need to take care of ourselves in order to be able to take care of others. It is similar to putting on your own air mask first on the airplane before you assist others. If we are completely drained, can we really help others? If we push ahead without taking some time for nurturing ourselves, what quality of help are we able to offer others?

Of course, the amount of time we can spend in nurturing ourselves depends on factors such as our stage of life, our responsibilities, and others who we may be caring for. It is a process of balancing and adjusting.

If you feel that your schedule doesn't allow you to take a long period of nurturing, you may decide to allocate a small amount each day. This may be adding additional time, or it may be starting from the beginning. Often, we have found our personal time slipping away one small block at a time until there is nothing left for us.

Adding this time back in begins in the same way, one small block at a time. Ten minutes here. Ten minutes there until we have found the balance that is comfortable and doable for us. It doesn't mean that we have to stick to a rigid schedule or do the same thing each day because this defeats the purpose of nurturing. It means doing what brings us the most joy and rejuvenation at the time. If it feels like a chore, then we have overdone it.

The type of nurturing that calls to you may depend on the way you spend the majority of your day. If you work in a traditional career, activities that nurture you may have a totally different focus than your work-day skills and tasks. If you are in a holistic career or one focused on spirituality, you may feel nurtured by similar activities, or you may want something that is a change. If you are in a caregiving role and do not work outside the home, this adds another dimension. Or, you may be free from your career path or responsibilities to others. The important thing is to do what calls to you at the moment.

One day we may decide to spend additional time in meditation. Or we may read a book, spend time in nature, take a long relaxing bath, do yoga, play with pets, or whatever calls to us at the time. We may decide just to be, rather than engaging in any activity.

In the past I would go from one activity to another because I felt that I would lose my momentum if I paused and took a break. Often, I would feel resentful that the activities and projects were keeping me from being true to myself even though they were things I enjoyed.

Finally, I knew I had to make a change. I began taking a few minutes of quiet time whenever I felt the prompt from my inner guidance. No matter what project I was working on, the quiet time took priority.

I was pleasantly surprised at the result.

Now I have found that when I spend those few minutes in quiet time, I feel nurtured and prepared for my work. This doesn't require me to abandon my plans, but it does help me to focus and receive guidance from the Universe for the rest of my day. As a result, I am more relaxed, focused, and productive.

When we add in those small things that make our heart sing, this is what will rejuvenate and nurture us. These are the ways we honor ourselves as the beautiful Beings that we are.

❖ ❖ ❖

Nurturing Yourself in the New Energy

~ Inspiration from The Angelic Realm ~

Beloved Ones,

You are continuing to experience many energy shifts that are bringing in new, higher-dimensional energy, and this is opening your awareness to new possibilities in the Universal Light. New realms and vistas are coming into your awareness.

The higher dimensional energy has a quality of refined Light. The particles of this Light are very fine and rarified. They have a quality of being very ethereal with infinite possibilities. They are calling to you and inviting you to experience this refined energy. They are reminding you of your true home. They are calling you to experience the Oneness of all of Creation. They are calling you to let your own energy field rise in refinement to incorporate this new energy.

Your personal energy field is enhanced when you nurture yourself. Nurturing yourself is no longer optional. It is crucial in the new energy.

Nurturing yourself in the new energy can help you to assimilate the higher dimensional frequencies. When you nurture yourself, you are surrounding yourself with the heart energy of the Divine Feminine. The Divine Feminine energy is loving, caring, compassionate, and understanding. It is longing to give you the nurturance you have provided to others for aeons. Now, it is time to give this nurturing energy of the Divine Feminine to yourself.

Surrounding yourself with the heart energy of the Divine Feminine enables you to relax and expand your consciousness to higher levels. Then, the new, higher dimensional energy can settle gently into your Being, and you begin to rise to higher levels.

The more often you assimilate the higher frequency energy, the more easily you can move between the dimensions. As you do this, you become aware, on a Soul-knowing level, that Love is the universal vibration of the spheres.

Nurturing yourself each day will help your vibration remain high. When you nurture yourself first, this keeps your Being filled with Light. This allows you to tap into Universal Love. As you are feeling this Love, you are able to be of greater service to humanity. It is hard to share with others what you do not first do for yourself. Therefore, nurturing yourself each day is not selfish. Quite the contrary, it is honoring your own Being by nurturing yourself first and then sharing this Universal Love with others.

The ways in which you decide to nurture yourself can range from time alone to being with others. It is highly personal depending on what makes your heart sing. Doing what makes you feel special restores your energy and helps you to nurture yourself.

It is the small, consistent nurturing of yourself that

can make your heart sing. Even a few small things each day can build a bridge of caring for yourself that will allow you to go throughout your day fulfilling other responsibilities more easily. When you know that you will be doing kind, nurturing things for yourself each day, your Being is more likely to remain filled with higher dimensional Light. It is an anticipation and joy when you appreciate and honor your Being.

One technique that you may wish to use to nurture yourself is to tune in to your Divine Spark, which connects you to All That Is. It is the eternal part of you that resides in your heart center. The more often you tune in to your Divine Spark, the more brightly it will shine. This allows you to receive and carry even more Universal Love and Light. Your own Being is singing and happy, and this Light radiates out to humanity, the planet, and the Universe.

This allows you to view events in your current surroundings from a higher perspective. You can more easily relate to others. You realize that everyone has a Divine Spark within and that this is what connects everyone in Oneness.

Another way to nurture yourself is to practice self-

appreciation. You can do this by focusing on your positive qualities. This is not done in a boastful manner. It is rather acknowledging those qualities that are part of who you are. This can be done privately in your quiet time.

These qualities may range from kindness to loyalty to being helpful to others. You may be open to new concepts and are a seasoned seeker on the spiritual path. Focusing on positive qualities can help to raise your vibration and keep your heart energy open to universal Love.

When you practice self-appreciation, this helps you keep your body full of nurturing energy. Then, you are able to extend this nurturing to others. You begin to rise to higher-dimensional levels and, in turn, help to lift the energy of those around you.

Beloveds, we are with you as you nurture yourself.

Know that you are greatly loved.

~ The Angelic Realm

Personal Quiet Time and Silence

—⚭—

As you are moving forward with assessing where you are on your path, you may want to pause and reflect on the importance of your personal quiet time and silence.

Silence breaks the normal, linear chain of thinking. Silence lifts you out of your established, accustomed patterns into a state where all possibilities exist – a state where the energy can be reshaped into your desired pattern.

Silence is the essence of unmanifested energy. When you enter into this state, you are allowing all potential possibilities to reveal themselves.

When you are feeling overwhelmed, rushed, and have a full schedule, taking quiet time for yourself is even more crucial. Even a brief time of silence allows you to tune out the outer noise of the opinions of others and what society expects and, instead, to turn inward to see how you are feeling about what is occurring and whether you resonate with it.

When you do this, you are much more likely to keep from saying "yes" to a request when you really want to say "no."

I have often experienced times when my schedule was overloaded. Even though I took full responsibility for this, the fact that I felt overwhelmed was still a reality. I had let myself fall into a trap of saying yes to many opportunities without fully assessing my schedule and how each activity fit in with my desired path.

Sometimes, I had said yes because I wanted to fit in with the crowd. At other times, the activity sounded like fun, or I thought it would help me on my path. As a result, I was overscheduled and overloaded.

Finally, I reached a point where I knew I needed to make a change. I began delaying giving an answer to requests until I thought about it overnight. The pause of delaying an answer gave me the opportunity to be in total silence at night – to tune in to my heart center and see if the potential activity made my heart sing, whether it was a good fit for my path, and whether I could comfortably fit it in my schedule.

After I began using this practice, I found that I

made much better decisions that allowed me to be true to myself.

The power of silence brings an inner awareness of who we are and our connection to Source. It prepares us for deciding the next step on our path and how to remain true to ourselves.

❖ ❖ ❖

The Power of Silence

~ Inspiration from the Angelic Realm ~

Beloved Ones,

The higher vibrational energy is continuing to reach your planet at the same time that you are progressing on your ascension path. You are making great strides as you determine what your next step is and how you wish it to look.

Pausing and taking time to observe the silence can yield many benefits at this point on your path.

As you incorporate the higher vibrational energy, you are becoming more inner directed in your decisions rather than listening to the many voices and opinions in the outer world. You are setting aside the outer noise in favor of your own inner counsel and connection to Universal wisdom.

The outer noise could be things such as television, radio, the opinions of friends, and even your own thoughts about what was previously important to you. You have reached a point in your journey where you are assessing your next step, and the outer noise may have become a distraction rather than a help.

While in the past you may have found great comfort in the outer situations, you may be experiencing an inner prompt that another mode is needed at this time.

You may be feeling that you need to take a temporary break from these things in order to regain your spiritual balance and determine the next step for you.

If you experience this inner prompt, you may wish to assess what is right for you to change temporarily. After your temporary hiatus from the outer situations, you can assess what you wish to add back.

Many times, the outer noise can block your attention from receiving what your guides and inner guidance are bringing you. If you always have activity and noise around you, focusing can sometimes be a challenge. Your own inner prompts may not be able to come through.

To remove the outer noise, you can begin in a mode that suits you. What works for others may not appeal to you, so choosing your own method is crucial. You may decide to take some time off from outer noise such as television, the opinions of others, or any activity that you define as outer noise.

You can consciously decide to set aside a time or several times each day when you are totally silent.

As you do this, consciously assess how you feel. Are you calmer? Can you tune in more easily to your own inner guidance and that of your guides?

At times you may become aware that your own thoughts are playing in your mind in a continuous loop. Thank the thoughts and let them pass through. They will eventually fade away when they find that they do not capture your attention.

Then you can experience inner stillness as well as the outer stillness around you. You are experiencing the power of silence.

You feel the peacefulness that resides there in the stillness. Your body and mind begin to relax. You may notice the gentle inflow and outflow of your breath, and you relax even more. You feel at one with All That Is. You recognize yourself as the spiritual Being that you are.

You are aware that you have a Divine role in the Cosmos and that you are in the right place at the right time for this awareness to occur.

In the silence, you can determine what is right for you. There is no judgment. It is you with your own inner guidance, your guides, and your connection with Source.

When you relax into this knowingness, the power of silence is your friend. It is there to guide you, assist you, and comfort you on your ascension journey.

Know that you are greatly loved.

~ The Angelic Realm

Maintaining a Calm Center

—————∞∞∞—————

As you continue to move forward as a seasoned traveler on your ascension path, you have probably realized the importance of maintaining a calm center.

A calm center helps you maintain your internal point of control and act from your own personal system of guidance rather than being unduly influenced by others. It is part of your command center that helps you stay on course with your intentions.

When you have set your current intentions for your path, they become programmed into your consciousness in much the same way as you program the guidance system in your car.

Maintaining a calm center allows us to access our own guidance to be sure we are moving forward on our desired direction for our path. It is the mechanism that helps us sort through the outer noise that we all encounter in daily life.

There are many things that can pull us off our intended path. They can range from things we really enjoy, such as watching a favorite television program or spending unplanned time in activities that catch our attention at the moment, to things we gave up some time ago, such as participating in groups that were right for us at the time but no longer call to us. Someone may invite us to go just to remember the old times of fun.

On the surface these activities may seem to be a good fit, but upon closer examination, they may no longer be the best use of our time for our new and revised intentions for our path. Deciding what to do can be a balancing act, especially as we rise to multidimensional levels.

When we maintain a calm center, we can more easily determine what is right for us at the present time. We are also more likely to remain calm when something unexpected arises, such as problems with our technology. We can look at the situation as a detached observer, make a decision, and take action more effectively when we aren't thrown off balance by what is happening. Maintaining a calm center builds up a reserve of inner calmness that we can draw on as needed.

You likely have your own techniques for building up this internal center of calmness. They may include meditation and quiet time, listening to relaxing music, or reading something inspirational. Whatever your favorite techniques are, the important thing is to do them regularly to keep your internal center calm. It is similar to recharging our cell phones to keep the battery charged and ready for use.

I have found that I can move forward more easily when I regularly practice the techniques that help me maintain a calm center. Some of my favorites are focusing on my breath several times a day, meditating, doing yoga, and spending quiet time. Whenever I feel myself becoming stressed, I realize that I need to increase the time doing the things that build up a reserve of peace and calm in my center. As I do this, I am able to move through my day more easily.

When we honor ourselves by doing the things that help us maintain a calm center, we can move forward with our stated intentions in a way in which we are being true to ourselves.

❖ ❖ ❖

Maintaining Your Calm Center of Peace

~ Inspiration from The Angelic Realm ~

Beloved Ones,

Maintaining a calm center of peace is essential with the increasing energetic frequencies. They are rising to a higher vibrational level, and they are offering you an opportunity for advancing to higher levels of awareness.

When the vibrational frequencies are increasing, conditions around you sometimes appear to be chaotic and unsettled. This is because when higher frequency energy interacts with lower frequency energy, there is a disruption in the established pattern. There may be portions of the two patterns that are not compatible, and a rearrangement must occur for the new energy to be integrated.

When you are aware of this process, you can rise above the outer circumstances and view them as a detached observer.

This process is much easier when you maintain a calm center of inner peace.

This center is your point of reference and retreat so that you can remain focused on your spiritual path.

It is the center that both grounds you and allows you to soar to the multidimensions. It acts as your anchor. When you have a secure sense with your calm center of inner peace, you are able to navigate throughout daily life and progress on your spiritual path.

Knowing that this is your center of reference enables you to return to a point of focus whenever needed.

It also connects you with the Higher Dimensions because you realize that you are more than your physical body and the immediate external conditions around you.

Your internal calm center contains your Divine Spark that connects you with All That Is and helps you realize the Oneness of all of creation.

With these realizations, outer circumstances can be put in perspective, and you can move throughout your day while remaining centered in the knowledge of your true nature as a spiritual Being.

Connecting with your calm center of peace begins with remembering that it is always there for you to have a restful oasis. You may wish to pause throughout the day to connect with it. This peacefulness resides in your heart center.

As soon as you turn your awareness inward to your heart center, you begin to relax and feel calmer. You can focus on your breath to help your mind and body relax. As you do this, you are turning your attention from outer circumstances to your inner center. The outer conditions are still there, but you have shifted your attention inward to a higher spiritual awareness. As you continue to focus on your heart center and observe your breath flowing gently in and out, you become more peaceful and relaxed.

As this occurs, you remember that you are a Being of Light. You are also aware that, in addition to your own advancement, you are here to play your part for highest good for all of humanity and the planet.

You may receive insights and ideas about your spiritual path that will allow you to continue to advance, and you can communicate more clearly with the Higher Dimensions.

This occurs more easily when you are in your calm center of inner peace. It acts as a foundation upon which you can rise and continue on your ascension path. You are able to rise to the Higher Dimensions on a strand of Light and return to the foundation of your calm center as you desire. This allows you to function as a multidimensional Being of Light.

The more you function at a multidimensional level, the more your consciousness expands. You may find yourself receiving glimpses of other dimensions and star systems along with increased insights from the Beings of Light on all levels, including the Angelic Realm and the Ascended Masters.

As you receive these insights, you are aware that maintaining your calm center of inner peace is your point of ascension consciousness. It is here that you ask for highest good. With this awareness, you include highest good as part of your intentions on your spiritual path. An aura of peace radiates out from you, and you are a Light for highest good.

Beloveds, we are happy that you are focusing on maintaining your calm center of inner peace.

Know that you are greatly loved.

~ The Angelic Realm

Inner Peace

—⟨∞⟩—

Inner peace is a desired state of being for many of us who are seasoned travelers on the spiritual path. It is the vibration that connects us with the Divine.

We have seen our journeys take many twists and turns as we have arrived at our current point. Each step has brought us insights and lessons that have helped us to develop into the beautiful multidimensional Beings that we are.

We know that we have progressed spiritually and that we have unique missions to accomplish. We have recognized when we needed to make changes in our path.

We have examined what we want and what no longer resonates with us. We have learned to recognize the signals of what makes our heart sing, and we continue to be true to ourselves in the present moment. We continue to refine our paths to be who we want to be and to carry out our missions for greatest good.

We are aware of the energetic components in designing the path we want. These things include co-creating from a multidimensional perspective, setting a clear intention, putting our intentions into motion, continuing to work with the Higher Beings, recognizing intentions as part of spiritual growth, staying focused, and expressing gratitude.

We have recognized that we are constantly evolving and that we will always be refining our path as we move forward. We have honored letting go of what no longer is a good fit for us in the present moment, and we have nurtured ourselves in whatever way feels right at the time. We have realized that quiet time and solitude allow us to maintain a calm center and to tune in to our deepest desires for spiritual fulfillment.

We are aware that being true to ourselves is an important part of inner peace. When we are true to ourselves, we are expressing our Divine heritage for our greatest good and for the highest good of all of humanity and the many galaxies and universes throughout the multidimensions.

As we continue on our ascension paths, we honor ourselves as beautiful Beings of Light by being true to ourselves.

Honor and celebrate yourself for being true to yourself on your path!

◆ ◆ ◆

Inner Peace and Your Ascension Path

~ Inspiration from The Angelic Realm ~

Beloved Ones,

You have made great progress on your ascension path. You have taken the steps of examining each aspect of your spirituality and how you can be of service for your greatest good and for the highest good of all.

For this, we honor you.

We are happy that you have called on us to work with you on this great journey.

As you know, there are unlimited possibilities for you as you continue on this great adventure of ascension and working with us in the Higher Realms.

There are worlds and opportunities beyond your wildest imagination.

Throughout this process, remaining true to

yourself is of utmost importance.

As you rise higher on the ascension spiral, your choices take on even more importance because the energy is of a higher and finer frequency. Your desires manifest even more rapidly due to this rarified vibration. Therefore, being true to yourself is crucial.

When you continue to set your intentions for what is most important to you, we are able to assist you in harnessing the higher energy to manifest what you want, especially when it is for highest good.

All of this begins from a point of inner peace.

When you stay in a state of inner peace, you are able to discern what is true for you at each point on your spiritual path. You are focused, and you can discern what is right for you at the present moment. You recognize when you have completed a certain point of learning and when it is time to move to the next higher level of understanding. As you do this, new vistas appear, and you are able to explore even greater possibilities.

The inner peace you experience as you are being true to yourself will allow you to rise to your highest aspirations on your spiritual journey.

Beloveds, it is an honor for us to work with you.

Know that you are greatly loved.

~ The Angelic Realm

Conclusion

—❧—

Being true to yourself is an ongoing process.

You are constantly evolving. You are not the same person you were last year, last week, yesterday, or even five minutes ago.

As you continue to refine your path to be true to yourself, remember the many stepping stones on your path.

You are a beautiful Being.

You have a unique mission.

Turn inward to listen to the song of your heart.

Do what makes your heart sing.

As a seasoned traveler on the spiritual path, you can access the multidimensional energy and see events from this perspective.

Setting a clear intention allows you to harness the

energy to shape the path of your dreams.

Putting your intentions into motion is an important part of manifesting your dreams.

The Higher Beings of Light are always here to work with you when you call on them.

Allow your intentions to be for your highest good and the greatest good of all.

Setting intentions for your spiritual growth helps you to progress on your ascension path.

Stay focused as you receive the higher dimensional energy.

Express gratitude at each step of your path to complete the loop of manifestation.

As you evolve, let go of those things that no longer serve you.

Remain in the present moment to be the most current version of yourself.

Be gentle with yourself.

Personal quiet time and silence can help you to tune in to your inner guidance and maintain a calm center.

Inner peace is a product of being true to yourself.

Be the beautiful Light that you are!

Above all, be true to yourself!

❖ ❖ ❖

About the Author

Linda Mary Robinson is an author, spiritual teacher, and speaker with an emphasis on personal development, spirituality, and metaphysics. She is a Messenger of Light for the Angelic Realm, the Divine Feminine, the Hathors, and other Higher Beings of Light. Her greatest work is inspiring people who are ready for the next level on their spiritual journey.

She established Personal Pathways of Light as a way to teach, honor, and share with others on their unique pathways of ascension. Her messages of wisdom teachings from Archangel Zadkiel and Lady Amethyst are included on her website www.PersonalPathwaysOfLight.com.

She speaks at spiritual and metaphysical events on topics such as being true to yourself, progressing to the next level of your spiritual development, and her pilgrimages to sacred sites. Upon request, she also presents seminars and interactive workshops on the wisdom teachings from the Angelic Realm.

Linda is the author of *Reflections on the Path: The Awakening,* in which she describes her own journey of spiritual growth and transformation from a traditional background to awakening to metaphysics and spirituality. It is available on Amazon and Kindle.

Linda has been a student of personal growth, spirituality, and metaphysics since 1978. She is certified in several modalities of spiritual growth and energy work.

Linda has a Master of Education Degree in Guidance and Counseling. In her previous career, she taught life skills to adults and youth in non-formal settings. She was also a volunteer on a crisis hotline.

A native of North Carolina, Linda has lived her adult life in the Hampton Roads area of Virginia, where she currently resides. She has traveled on pilgrimages to sacred sites in Bolivia, England, Scotland, Ireland, Egypt, Greece, Israel, Jordan, Canada, Peru, and the United States.

~ Contact Linda at ~
Linda@PersonalPathwaysOfLight.com

Made in the USA
Las Vegas, NV
25 August 2022